HAPPINESS IS A CHOICE

Recommended by

ED WHEAT,
author of *Intended for Pleasure:*

"As a family physician and certified sex therapist, I have found there is nothing so hindering to the ability to express and receive love as depression in its many forms. Dr. Minirth and Dr. Meier offer a precise and perceptive overview of this trying condition and the practical medical/Biblical solutions which can bring hope to the depressed person and to those who love him. *Happiness is a Choice* adds a much-needed dimension to the entire field of psychiatry."

JAMES C. DOBSON,
Associate Clinical Professor of Pediatrics,
USC School of Medicine:

" . . . an excellent book . . . to help Christians cope with the miseries of depression. Drs. Minirth and Meier have described the disorder in non-technical language, explaining not only causes and cures, but also offering encouragement and hope to those who need it most. I recommend [this book] enthusiastically . . . ."

FLOYD F. McCALLUM,
Professor of Psychology, Houghton College:

"The analyses of depression, its causes, types of personalities, and recommendations for overcoming [depression] are cogent and persuasive. I am especially pleased with the integration of psychology and Biblical principles with the emphasis on hope for all who will carefully follow their recommended program for overcoming depression."

LLOYD M. PERRY,
Director, Doctor of Ministry Program,
Trinity Evangelical Divinity School:

"The technical thoroughness and accuracy combined with the biblical orientation make this book one which both pastors and laymen will appreciate . . . a healthy combination of faith and science."

JAMES R. SLAUGHTER,
Pastor, Calvary Baptist Church, Salinas, California:

"I have found this volume to be most helpful in my own counseling ministry, but perhaps more significant, extremely profitable in my own life. With the help of Minirth and Meier I have learned things about myself which I trust will make me a more understanding and effective pastor, and a more useful servant of Jesus Christ."

GLENN O'NEAL,
Dean, Talbot Theological Seminary:

" . . . a vital contribution to the field of Pastoral Counseling . . . in terms a non-professional can understand."

HAPPINESS IS A CHOICE

A Manual on the Symptoms, Causes, and Cures of Depression

Frank B. Minirth
and
Paul D. Meier

BAKER BOOK HOUSE
Grand Rapids, Michigan

ISBN: 0-8010-6086-9, cloth
0-8010-6087-7, paper

Library of Congress Catalog Card
Number: 78-062442

Seventh printing, November 1980

Printed in the United States of America

To our wives
Mary Alice Minirth
and
Jan Meier
who make happiness
a much easier choice

and to
our parents
who nourished us
in love, discipline,
and Christian principles

Acknowledgments

We wish to acknowledge the following friends, who have contributed to the writing of this book through their prayers. They have also contributed indirectly by the examples they have been of Christian men and women living lives of genuine love, joy, and peace. For them, happiness is a choice and a reality:

Dave and Nancy Brown, Mel and Bettye Goodenough, Rich and Linda Case, Tex and Dottie Driver, Frank and Kathy Wichern, States and Myra Skipper, Bill and Mary Goodin, Dave and Carolyn Peterson, John and Carolyn Best, Dave and Dee Deardorff, Henry and Melinda Harris, Duncan and Anne Jensby, Rick and Emily Efird, Ed and Karinna Keplinger, Freddie and Linda McRae, Ray and Cindy Mummert, Pat and Barbara McGee, Gary and Diane Walter, David and Becky Young, Townsend and Debby Dunn, Scott and Peggy Dye, Dwight and Hilde Johnson, Frank and Mary Pat Parma, Mildred Peterson, Madora Cushman, Bill and Phyllis Roush, Jerry and Jean Ryan, David and Connie Schroeder, Dennis and Sharon Simonetta, Mark and Rhonda Verkler, Haddon and Bonnie Robinson, Walter Bodine, Duane Litfin, John Reed, Jim Kutnow, Mike Cocoris, Ross Bannister, Waylon Ward, and Tokunboh Adeyemo.

We also want to thank our students at Dallas Theological Seminary, whose questioning and commitment to Scripture sharpen us academically and spiritually.

We also want to thank our friends who typed our original manuscript: Nancy Brown, Bettye Goodenough, Sally Brantmeier, and Mary Ann Johnson.

Foreword

I often recall a colleague, an eminent and very well-known psychiatrist, who entrusted his daughter to my care after she had attempted suicide. In a letter to me, my colleague wrote that he was not a believer, but his daughter was, and that he thought a believer like me was best equipped to help her resolve her difficulties.

My colleague was much more of an expert than I, who am only a simple general practitioner. In a way, then, this was a matter of an act of faith regarding faith. Thus, even an unbelieving doctor may consider faith to be a factor in recovery.

How does it happen that there are so many depressed individuals among the most fervent believers? And also, how does it happen that so often their faith, which (as my colleague thought) could be a factor in recovery, appears to further complicate their case, because they reproach themselves for their depression, as if it were a matter of lack of faith?

We see how these relationships between spiritual life and psychological health are subtle and delicate. They must be envisioned in their complexity. We must take account of the importance both of religious life and of the pathological phenomena which science studies.

Too often there is a tendency to place faith and science in opposition to each other instead of joining them. Some misjudge the role of faith in destiny, and others misjudge the role of maladies which strike believers as well as unbelievers and which science discloses. The sick and the healthy need to be enlightened on this double aspect of life.

It is the merit of this book by my two American colleagues that they have dealt with this double aspect of life in a manner so serious and clear that it is accessible to everyone. Here is a book which will help all depressed individuals to better understand themselves and thus to contribute to their own recovery. But this book will also help those who are healthy to better understand the depressed, who so often have the feeling of being misunderstood or misjudged by those who are healthy. This will in turn be favorable to the recovery of the depressed.

Anyone who reads this book will gain a better knowledge of the laws of life which are divine, so that he may better conform to those laws.

What is it that science studies, if not the laws of nature, the laws established by the Creator over his creation? And the first law of God is love! Like the authors of this book, I hope that every reader finds in these pages an opportunity to approach both God and good health.

Geneva, June 23, 1978 — Paul Tournier

Contents

Inner Reflections

I would like
to initiate the reader
on his or her journey through this book
by breaking tradition and sharing
some of my personal, innermost
reflections. As I write this
I am sitting calmly in
a waiting area at the Dallas/Fort Worth
Airport. As I gaze out
the windows I see the large cumulus
clouds gently floating
by as the airplanes mechanically
come and go.
I feel an inner joy and excitement.
I feel at peace with God,
at peace with my wife and children, and
at peace with the friends I love
so dearly. And yet, as I

am looking around this waiting area and analyzing (as we psychiatrists love to do) the people sitting around me, I have a somewhat different inner feeling. As I search for ways to describe it, I think of the word *angst*—a term present-day German philosophers and theologians are tossing around. *Angst* is a type of undefinable inner anxiety. As I look around right now and think about the condition of my fellow man en masse, I feel *angst*. In my practice of psychiatry I counsel many individuals from that mass of humanity; I have come to understand the repressed fears, insecurities, and anger within many of them, sometimes even hidden behind smiling faces. I understand and I empathize. In fact, I not only empathize, I hurt for them deep within. I want them to know the things I have learned that have brought me great personal joy and inner peace. That is why Dr. Frank Minirth and I feel compelled to write this book—to share what we have learned with you, the reader, in hopes that you will in turn pass it on to others you love.

Many years ago I read a very thought-provoking statement made by Abraham Lincoln: "Most people are about as happy as they choose to be." I couldn't agree with him more. Lincoln should know. He went through much anguish in his life—the death of his fiancée, lost elections, the Civil War, and other major disappointments. At one period of his life he was so depressed he considered suicide. But Lincoln chose to overcome his depression. He chose to be happy and obtained inner joy and peace in those last years before he fell victim to the bullet of a hostile fellow man.

Before you decide to agree or disagree with Lincoln's assertion that "most people are about as happy as they choose to be," or with the authors' assertion that "happiness is a choice," let me explain what the title we have selected means. My associate and I have a combined post-high school education totaling twenty-six years. During that time we thoroughly researched man's psychology, physiology, anatomy, mentality, and spirituality. We have also exercised our psychotherapeutic skills on hundreds of patients. Both of us can say with a deep inner conviction that a majority of human beings do *not* have the inner peace and joy about which I am thinking. We are also convinced that all human beings are capable of having this inner joy and peace if only they will choose it *and* follow the right path to obtain it.

It is difficult for many laymen to comprehend that anyone would choose unhappiness and depression over peace and happiness, but many people do so for a variety of reasons of which they are unaware. Some choose unhappiness to punish themselves for guilt feelings. Others choose unhappiness to manipulate their mates and friends by enlisting their sympathies. Other inner motivations for remaining depressed will be analyzed later in this book.

As a further point of clarification, Dr. Minirth and I are convinced that many people do choose happiness but still do *not* obtain it. The reason for this is that even though they choose to be happy, they seek for inner peace and joy in the wrong places. They seek for happiness in materialism and do not find it. They seek for joy in sexual prowess but end up with fleeting pleasures and bitter long-term disappointments. They seek inner fulfillment by obtaining positions of power in corporations, in government, or even in their own families (by exercising excessive control), but they remain unfulfilled. I have had millionaire businessmen come to my office and tell me they have big houses, yachts, condominiums in Colorado, nice children, a beautiful mistress, an unsuspecting wife, secure corporate positions—and suicidal tendencies. They have everything this world has to offer except one thing—inner peace and joy. They come to my office as a last resort, begging me to help them conquer the urge to kill themselves. Why? The answers are not simple. The human mind and emotions are a very complex, dynamic system. In this book we will do the best we can to summarize some of these complexities in layman's terminology and offer guidelines, step by step, for obtaining lasting inner happiness—*if you choose it.*

Now I am floating in a large jetliner thirty-five thousand feet in the air and high above those enormous cumulus clouds I watched float by a short time ago. I am heading for Los Angeles to address a weekend retreat of physicians and their wives. I have been asked to teach them what I know about sources of emotional pain in physicians and their families. They are taking this weekend off from their busy schedules to find out how to obtain inner peace and joy. I respect them for that. Physicians and dentists have the highest suicide rates in our current American culture. They are overwhelmed with pressures which they perceive as being external. In reality, their overwhelming pressures are primarily from within—from perfectionistic, masochistic, self-critical inner drives and insecurities. Many of them have an enormous fear of failure and a strong need to rescue the world from illness and death. That is why Schulz, in his "Peanuts" comic strip, refers to the M.D. degree as the "M. Deity" degree. Most physicians (including Dr. Minirth and myself) go into medicine because of their compassion for a suffering mankind. At least, that is their *conscious* motivation for entering medicine. Many physicians, unfortunately, experience a phenomenon known as "burn-out"—a loss of human compassion due to the strenuous demands and regimentation of medical school, internship, residency, and private practice. Many of my current psychiatric patients are fellow physicians from other specialties who are depressed and suffering from considerable emotional pain.

As I fly over the beautiful western states between Texas and California, I am feeling *angst* for those physicians and their wives waiting for me in Los Angeles. I am pondering not only on what I am going to share with the physicians and their wives at the retreat, but also on what I can share with the readers of this book. In regard to the latter I see two primary tasks lying ahead of me. My larger task (though this may seem incredible) is to persuade the reader to give up his depression and choose happiness. This sounds ridiculous to many people who do not understand the complexity and depravity of human nature. But it is true, nevertheless! Depression meets many unconscious neurotic needs. When patients come to me and tell me they have been depressed for many years and that they have had enough of their depression, we sit down together and analyze what rewards they have unconsciously been getting by unwittingly choosing years of depression. The unconscious motives vary from person to person, but they invariably revolve around the emotion of anger—repressed anger—and holding grudges against self, others, or God (these concepts will be discussed later in this book). After analyzing *why* they are depressed, I attempt to persuade my patients to choose happiness.

The second task is to persuade the reader to commit his life to the *correct course* for obtaining inner love, happiness, and peace. People get very set in their ways. Even when they have tried their ways for twenty or thirty years with no lasting results, they still cling to their childhood behavior patterns. Many alcoholics, for example, are surprised to find out that when they give up drinking and become responsible family men, their complaining (and controlling) wives divorce them and marry another alcoholic. I see this repeatedly! Our brains are very much like complex computers, as behavioral research is demonstrating today. Most people choose to continue in the behavior patterns their parents correctly or incorrectly programmed into their computer-brains in early childhood. In an earlier book (*Christian Child-Rearing and Personality Development*, Baker, 1977), I fully demonstrated and documented my belief that approximately 85 percent of our behavior patterns and attitudes are firmly entrenched by age six. I am *not* saying that we are permanently locked into those childhood behavior patterns and there is nothing we can do about it—it is just that most humans *ignorantly choose to* stay locked into those early childhood behavior patterns and world-views. Thank God that He created within us a human will. When He created us in His image, He gave us a will—an ability to choose. Without the power of the will, the efforts of psychotherapy or even writing this book would be worthless. I am hoping and praying that you—the reader—will exercise your God-given will in choosing some new, health-producing attitudes and behavior patterns. Your happiness is my goal. But I have no power at all to make anybody happy except myself. All I can do is to persuade the reader that he should choose happiness and to point out what I believe to be the correct path to obtain it. It is then up to him to choose and follow that path.

Paul D. Meier, M.D.

PART ONE

What Is Depression?

1

Who Gets Depressed?

Then the Lord said to Cain,
Why are you angry? And why has
your countenance fallen? (Gen. 4:6).

A young lady
whom we had never seen before
was waiting in our reception room.
She was invited into one of
our offices and asked about the
nature of her problem.
Immediately she burst into tears
and related how depressed she felt.
She said she felt blue,
sad, hopeless, and helpless.
Life was not worth living.
In short, she felt
very anxious and desperate.
She had been praying

that we would be able to help her, and her tone sounded as though she felt we were the last hope.

This young lady was suffering from America's number one health problem—depression. As psychiatrists we see more people suffering from depression than from all other emotional problems put together. A *majority* of Americans suffer from a serious, clinical depression sometime during their lives. At the present time, one American in twenty is medically diagnosed as suffering from depression.[1] Of course, many, many more are depressed but never receive help. According to one estimate about twenty million persons in America between the ages of eighteen and seventy-four are currently depressed.[2] Depression is the leading cause of suicide; in fact about 15 percent of those people who are significantly depressed will eventually commit suicide.[3] Suicide is the tenth leading cause of death in America today, and it is the second leading cause of death among college students.[4] Depression occurs two times more often in females than males, and it occurs three times more often in higher socio-economic groups.[5] Money definitely does not buy happiness! Depression occurs most often in the fourth and fifth decades of life, but may occur during any stressful period from infancy to old age.[6]

Depression is a vague term. Laymen use it to describe a wide spectrum of behavior—anything from a mild swing of mood to psychosis. We all fit into that spectrum somewhere and to some extent our degree of depression versus happiness varies from hour to hour and day to day. As psychiatrists, we treat people who are "clinically depressed"—that is, so depressed that they are having physiological symptoms.

Depression has been discussed since the time of Job to the present. Ever since the symptoms were first recorded, they have remained the same. The Bible records the depressive symptoms of such men as Job, Moses, Elijah, David, and Jeremiah. In the 1600s, Richard Burton wrote a classic book on depression—*The Anatomy of Melancholia*. In this century, well-known authors such as Freedman, Solomon, Patch, Eaton, Peterson, Arieti, Kolb and others have described in detail the symptoms of depression.[7] Many of the symptoms they have described are listed in the next chapter.

Who gets depressed? At some period of life, nearly everyone does! Our strong contention, however, is that suffering from the emotional pains of a clinical depression is a totally unnecessary, totally avoidable experience. To avoid it, one must choose happiness as a way of life and follow the right path to obtain it.

2

What Are the Symptoms of Depression?

Depression is
a devastating illness
that affects the total being—
physically, emotionally, and spiritually.
The emotional pain of depression is more
severe than the physical pain
of a broken leg.
Unlike a broken leg, however,
the pains of depression come on much
more gradually.
Many men and women are currently suffering
from numerous symptoms of depression
without even realizing
that they suffer from depression
rather than from
some purely physical illness.
The symptoms of clinical depression
fall into five major categories:

sad affect, painful thinking, physical symptoms, anxiety, and delusional thinking.[1]

Sad Affect (Moodiness)

One major symptom of depression is a sad affect (or moodiness). An individual suffering from depression has a sad facial expression. He looks depressed. He either cries often or feels like it. His eyes are cast down and sad. The corners of his mouth droop. His forehead is wrinkled. He looks tired, discouraged, and dejected. His features are strained. As the depression progresses, he gradually loses interest in his personal appearance. Sometimes men even stop shaving and women stop putting on their make-up. Thus, the seriously depressed individual frequently appears untidy. Even if he tries to hide his depression by smiling, it still shows. In fact, many depressed individuals have what is known as a *smiling depression*. Many men and women smile inappropriately to cover up the sad or angry feelings within.

Painful Thinking

A second major symptom of depression is painful thinking. As surely as a broken arm is painful physically, so the thinking of a depressed individual is *painful emotionally*. Many persons who have experienced both severe physical and emotional pain have stated emphatically that emotional pain is worse than physical pain. They would prefer broken bones to a broken heart! The depressed individual is very *introspective* in a self-derogatory way. He ruminates a great deal over past mistakes. He often feels guilty, even when innocent. He may feel responsible when he is not. He feels at fault when blameless. He worries excessively over all kinds of wrongs in the past, both real and imagined. His thoughts are self-debasing. He has a negative *self-concept*. He has an exaggerated view of his problems and frequently blames himself for all of his problems (some depressed individuals go to the opposite extreme, however, and inappropriately blame others for all their problems as they wallow in self-pity). He tends to view himself as being deficient in qualities that he considers important, such as popularity, intelligence, or spiritual maturity. He feels blue, *sad, helpless, worthless,* and *hopeless.* (In fact, *75 percent of depressives feel they will never recover.*) He often feels deprived of emotional support and thus feels empty and *lonely.* He craves affection and reassurance from others, but often his deep-seated hostility frustrates his purposes. He is filled with remorse for imagined wrongs, both recent and remote. He is unhappy and *pessimistic.* He may become petulant and distrustful. His every experience is combined with his mental pain. He is preoccupied with himself. He is *self-possessed.* He is absorbed with a few topics of melancholic nature. He anticipates nonacceptance from others and *feels rejected and unloved,* usually significantly out of proportion to reality. He is so occupied with himself and his ruminations that his attention, concentration, and memory are impaired. He feels anxious and perplexed. To him the future is gloomy. He experiences a low energy level and a sense of futility.

As we have stated above, the painful thinking often centers around guilt. The guilt may be true guilt, but often for the depressed individual false guilt is also a significant problem. He feels guilty when innocent. He feels guilty for many minor mistakes and wrongs. Most individuals have suffered from guilt for brief periods of time after doing something wrong (the only exception is a sociopath or a criminal). Thus, most know how painful guilt is for even a brief period. Imagining how painful it would be to live with a constant haunting guilt can help one to understand how miserable the depressed individual feels. He has guilt which he thinks he cannot escape.

The painful thinking of the depressed individual centers around taking on responsibility for acts and events which, realistically, are outside of his control. This may have its genesis in man's need to feel important. The depressed individual has an overwhelming sense of inadequacy and has feelings of worthlessness. He feels as though he is *a nobody*—a zero. However, he refuses to be a nobody. He surely cannot be a zero if he is responsible for a great many events and acts—if so much hinges on him. Thus, in a warped sort of way, his feelings of overwhelming responsibility protect him unconsciously from his feelings of worthlessness. They give him a great sense of power. In many ways He becomes *omnipotent* as a reaction against his true inner feelings of inadequacy and emotional *impotence.*

The depressed individual is characterized by motivational disturbances. That is, he *lacks motivation*. He loses interest in the type of activities in which he was previously involved. He begins to avoid people and wishes to be left alone. He loses his sense of humor. He becomes *indecisive*. Eventually, he becomes suicidal.

Physical Symptoms

A third major category of the symptoms of clinical depression includes the physical symptoms, which are known by medical doctors as the "physiological concomitants of depression." Actual biochemical changes involving the brain amines take place in the human nervous system during clinical depressions. These biochemical changes have various physical results: The body movements of the depressed individual usually decrease. The quality of his *sleep* is affected. He may have difficulty falling asleep at night, but more often he suffers from waking up too early in the morning. After waking up early he has difficulty going back to sleep. This is a frequent occurrence. Initially, rather than sleeping too little, he may sleep too much. His *appetite* is also often affected. He either eats too much or too little (usually too little). Thus, he may have either significant *weight loss or weight gain*. He may suffer from diarrhea, but more frequently from *constipation*. In women, the menstrual cycle may stop entirely for months, or it may be irregular. There is often a loss of *sexual interest*. The depressed individual may suffer from tension *headaches* or complain of tightness in his head. Along with *slow body movements*, he may have a stooped posture and seem to be in a stupor. He may have gastrointestinal disturbances. He may have a slow metabolic rate. He may suffer from a *dry mouth*. A *rapid heartbeat* and heart palpitations are fairly common. These physiological changes scare most individuals into hypochondriasis (an overconcern with physical illnesses). Many erroneously become convinced that they have cancer, or hypoglycemia, or a nutritional disorder. Actually, they would *prefer* to have a physical illness in order to save face. They hate to admit that they have psychological conflicts, which they view as weakness. Out of over one hundred patients who came to us thinking they had hypoglycemia, only one of them actually had borderline low blood sugars as determined by a six-hour glucose tolerance test.

Anxiety or Agitation

A fourth major symptom of depression is anxiety or agitation. Anxiety and depression usually occur together. The depressed individual feels anxious and often is more *irritable* than usual. Also, as depression increases, so does agitation. The depressed individual feels tense and has difficulty sitting still.

Delusional Thinking

A fifth major symptom that *can* occur in very severe depressions is *delusional thinking*. It differs from painful thinking only in degree—the delusional thinker is clearly out of touch with reality. His delusions involve either notions of persecution (e.g., he thinks people are out to get him) or grandiose assumptions (e.g., he thinks God has given him some special gift or insight). He may have auditory hallucinations—he hears voices that are often condemning and accusing in nature. The voices, of course, are not really there. He may also have *visual hallucinations*—he sees things that no one else sees. He may misinterpret these as visions from God. If he is treated soon after his break with reality, he is usually restored to normality, once again thinking clearly and happy with life. In such cases one or two months of hospitalization may be needed, with daily psychotherapy, antipsychotic and antidepressant medications, and encouragement. Unfortunately, some persons do become permanently psychotic.

In summary, a true clinical depression is a complex, painful disorder involving our total being—mind, body, and spirit. There can be a wide range of severity—from a sad affect and painful thinking all the way to complete loss of contact with reality (a psychotic break) in order to compensate for the extreme pain of reality. Most clinical depressions do *not* reach the psychotic stage. However, most clinical depressions do include a sad affect, painful thinking, physical symptoms (the physiological concomitants of depression), and anxiety (or agitation). If these symptoms disable the individual biologically and socially, he has a depressive neurosis. Anyone can be cured of a depressive neurosis if he becomes actively involved in good-quality professional psychotherapy. If the depressed individual has considerable anxiety along with his sad affect, painful thinking, and psychomotor retardation (slow body movements, but with periods of restlessness), he has agitated depression. This is also totally curable. However, if the depressed individual in addition has delusional thinking or hallucinations, he has a psychotic depression. Psychotic depressions are usually curable if caught fairly early, although they are much more difficult to treat. Some psychotic depressions worsen and become lifelong schizophrenic disorders which are incurable at present. It is our fervent hope that medical science may come up with some breakthroughs soon so that even "incurable" schizophrenics may someday be restored to total health.

A Self-Rating Depression Scale

Anyone who answers "true" to a majority of the following statements is almost certainly depressed and should seek professional assistance before the depression worsens.

1. I feel like crying more often now than I did a year ago.
2. I feel blue and sad.
3. I feel hopeless and helpless a good part of the time.
4. I have lost a lot of my motivation.
5. I have lost interest in things I once enjoyed.
6. I have had thoughts recently that life is just not worth living.
7. My sleep pattern has changed of late. I either sleep too much or too little.
8. I am losing my appetite.
9. I am too irritable.
10. I am anxious of late.
11. I have less energy than usual.

12. Morning is the worst part of the day.
13. I find myself introspecting a lot.
14. When I look at myself in the mirror, I appear to be sad.
15. My self-concept is not very good.
16. I worry much about the past.
17. I have more physical symptoms (headaches, upset stomach, constipation, rapid heartbeat, etc.) than I did a year ago.
18. I believe people have noticed that I do not function as well at my job as I did in the past.

3

Is Suicide a Sin?

Depression is
a leading cause of suicide.
Suicide is the tenth leading cause
of death in the United States;
it accounts for twenty-four thousand
deaths annually.[1]
A suicidal death occurs about every
twenty minutes, and there are
ten unsuccessful attempts for
every successful one.[2]
In the world as a whole,
the suicide rate seems to be increasing,
with five hundred thousand
being reported annually.[3]

Suicide is
uniquely a human problem.
Animals may kill other animals,

but they do not kill themselves. *Only man kills himself.*[4] It must be remembered, however, that not all suicide threats are genuine.

Case Study: Mrs. P's chief complaint was depression. She stated she wanted to commit suicide and because of that statement was admitted to the hospital. The next day she said she was no longer depressed. The dramatic quality of her story and gestures was noted during the mental evaluation. Rather than displaying the usual symptoms of depression (sad affect, guilt, physical symptoms, and anxiety), she appeared dramatic, dressed somewhat seductively, and felt no appreciable guilt. She gave a life history of a behavior pattern characterized by being emotional, excitable, overreactive, immature, attention-seeking, self-centered, manipulative, naive, impressionable, and dependent. These characteristics are typical of a person with a hysterical personality disorder. Instead of a depressive neurosis, then, Mrs. P. had a hysterical personality disorder. As such cases often do, she had represented her chief complaint as depression. Her threatened suicide was just that—a threat. Often these hysterical persons will manipulate others by their threat of suicide. Subsequent history revealed she was trying to manipulate her husband.

People who threaten suicide should be taken seriously, even though most suicide threats are merely manipulative. It is not true that people who threaten suicide never do so.[5] In fact, over 10 percent of the persons who make a suicide gesture eventually do commit suicide. Most people who commit suicide have warned someone of their intentions. Suicide is more frequent among the divorced, the widowed, and the higher socioeconomic groups.[6] It is also common among single adult males.[7] Women attempt suicide about five times more frequently than men; however, twice as many men are successful in the attempt.[8] The reason for this is that men tend to use more violent means to commit suicide and do not use suicide as a manipulative gesture as often as women do. People of all religious denominations commit suicide. In the college-age student, suicide is the second leading cause of death, rating second only to accidents. Every three minutes someone "attempts" suicide, and every twenty minutes someone succeeds.[9]

Potential suicides often share common characteristics or

experiences. There are ten warning signs of individuals most likely to attempt suicide:[10]

1. Individuals with intense emotional pain, as seen in depression.
2. Individuals with intense hopeless feelings.
3. Single white males over forty-five years of age.
4. Individuals with a prior history of a suicide attempt, and individuals who have warned others of their suicidal intentions. Of any ten people who commit suicide, eight have given definite warning.
5. Individuals with severe health problems.
6. Individuals who have experienced a significant loss of some kind—death of a spouse, loss of a job, etc.
7. Individuals who have made a specific suicide plan. The process builds as follows: Fleeting thoughts of suicide are followed by a serious consideration of suicide, which is followed by an actual attempt.
8. Individuals with chronic self-destructive behavior (such as alcoholism).
9. Individuals with an intense need to achieve.
10. Individuals with an excess of disturbing life events within the last six months.

Suicide is a terrible thing for several reasons. First, most people who commit suicide do so when they are not seeing things realistically. They would not commit suicide if they saw the true nature of the situation and realized that their problem was only temporary and solvable. After two months of therapy, patients who were formerly suicidal are amazed that they were actually considering suicide in the past. Secondly, the effects of suicide on the surviving children, other relatives, and friends are devastating. Children wrongly blame themselves for the suicide of a parent; they are also more likely to follow their parent's example by giving up on life and committing suicide when as adults they find themselves in difficult situations. Finally, suicide is a sin just as murder is a sin. "Thou shalt not kill" applies to our own lives as well as the lives of others. Suicide is never God's will!

Only seven suicides are listed in the Scriptures: Abimelech (Judges 9:54), Samson (Judges 16:30), Saul (I Samuel 31:14), Saul's armor bearer (I Samuel 31:5), Ahithophel (II Samuel 17:23), Zimri (I Kings 16:18), and Judas (the Gospels). None of the men who committed suicide was at that time acting in accordance with the will of God.

4

Are Grief Reactions the Same as Depression?

Every human being
suffers significant losses and reversals,
such as the death of a loved one,
the death of a favorite pet,
a business failure, rejection by a fiancé,
rejection by a medical school, the
loss of an arm or leg in a car accident,
the discovery of an incurable illness.
Whenever any human being suffers
a significant loss or reversal,
he goes through all five
stages of grief. Some mature individuals
go through them more quickly than
others. Grief reactions are *not*
clinical depressions.
However, a grief reaction can
turn into a clinical depression if a
person is weighed

down for too long a period in the second or third stage.

Stage 1: Denial

The individual refuses momentarily to believe this is really happening to him. This stage usually does not last very long.

Case Study: Jane was a five-year-old girl who was very attached to her father. One night while sleeping with her he had a heart attack. An ambulance came to take him to the hospital. When he was being removed from his bed, he promised Jane he would return. However, he died at the hospital. Jane was told of her father's death, but made use of massive denial techniques and continued for several years after her father's death to look for him in closets and under the bed. Even into her teen-age years Jane occasionally hallucinated that her father had walked into her room to say a kind word to her. She was weighed down in the denial stage of grief. It took her two years of weekly psychotherapy (from age fourteen to sixteen) to get out of it completely.

Stage 2: Anger Turned Outward

The second stage that all of us experience whenever we suffer a significant loss is an angry reaction toward someone other than ourselves. We even feel anger toward the person who died, even though he had no choice in the matter. This *always* happens when a young child loses one of his parents due to death or divorce, for instance. This is a normal human reaction. This stage almost always includes some anger toward God for allowing the loss to occur. Our anger toward God is often repressed so rapidly that we are not aware of it.

Case Study: Mrs. C. received counseling for two years after her divorce. She was still sad and depressed. Her grief reaction had turned into a long-standing depression. After thorough analysis, it was clear that she was still angry at God for allowing the divorce to occur and for not forcing her husband to straighten out his life. She denied this and expressed anger toward the psychiatrist for even insinuating that she might feel angry toward God. She had been quite religious in her youth. Accordingly, the thought that she might feel anger toward God made her afraid. Asked if she had ever practiced daily devotions and prayer, she responded that she had for many years—ever since she had accepted Christ as her Savior. But when asked if she was still having daily devotions, she hesitated for a moment and then said no. She had never really decided to quit having devotions, but had simply "got out of that habit about two years ago." On reflection she realized that she quit relating intimately to God at the same period of time that she gave up on her husband. She became acutely aware of her repressed anger toward God and wept, asking Him to forgive her. She was soon over her depression and relating intimately with God again.

Stage 3: Anger Turned Inward

After the reality of the significant loss or reversal is accepted and the grieving person has reacted angrily toward God and whomever else he holds responsible, the grieving person begins to feel quite guilty. The guilt is usually a combination of true guilt and false guilt. (For a discussion of true and false guilt, see pp. 69-73.) The grieving one feels some true guilt for holding a grudge against God and others. In Ephesians 4:26, the apostle Paul tells us that we can get angry without sinning, but that we should never let the sun go down on our wrath (that is, we should not hold grudges past bedtime). In other words, it is all right to get angry when we suffer a significant loss. Anger is an automatic human response. But somehow, with God's help, we must forgive whomever we feel anger toward by bedtime, whether they deserve our forgiveness or not. God wants us to forgive others and ourselves for our own good because if we hold grudges, we will eventually become clinically depressed. So the grieving person feels some legitimate guilt, for he is holding grudges and that is a sin.

The grieving person also begins at this point to ruminate over his own mistakes which may have contributed to the significant loss or reversal. He has a tendency at this point to absurdly blame himself for everything. Hindsight is always better than foresight; he can see in hindsight things he could have done that *may* have helped prevent the loss. He turns all his anger and grudges inward onto himself. Instead of confessing his true errors to God and forgiving himself for not having perfect foresight, he holds a grudge against himself and begins to punish himself through self-critical thoughts. Most people work through this stage fairly quickly (within a week or two) and go on to stage four. However, if the grieving person stays for very long in this anger-turned-inward stage, his grief will surely become a clinical depression which could take months to work through in therapy.

Case Study: Mrs. B. was a pastor's wife who came for therapy because she was depressed, anxious, and suicidal. Her blood pressure kept climbing upward and upward to a dangerous level. Her father had died one year prior to her decision to seek psychiatric help. In therapy it was discovered that she was weighed down in stage three of grieving over her father's death one year before. She felt guilty that she had not said "good-bye" or "I love you" to her father. She had also been angry at her father about some things and now felt very guilty about holding grudges against a man who had died. When someone dies, we tend to forget his bad points and shudder at the thought of being angry at a dead person. Her introverted anger was not only depressing her, but also driving her blood pressure up to a point where she could easily have died of a stroke. Using a Gestalt technique, her psychiatrist pretended to be her dead father and encouraged her to tell him all the emotions and thoughts she had bottled up inside. She refused at first because of fear of her own emotions, but was finally persuaded to do so. As usual, it was difficult to begin, but once she did, her good-byes and feelings of love, anger, and guilt came pouring forth along with many tears. Twenty minutes later she was relieved of all the emotions she had bottled up inside for over a year. Within a week her depression was lifted and her blood pressure was back to normal—and stayed that way.

Stage 4: Genuine Grief

This is probably the most important stage and a vitally necessary one. Whenever we suffer a significant loss or reversal, it is very important—for men as well as women—to have a good cry. Our culture encourages most men and some women to be stoic—to hold in their feelings and show how "strong" they are by not crying (not even at a funeral). Was Joseph weak when he wept over his father's death? Was Jesus Christ our Lord weak when He wept over the loss of his friend Lazarus? Of course not! Weeping over a significant loss is both human and godly. Not grieving can lead to a low-grade depression that can last for many years. Your dead loved one may be joyful in heaven now, but you will still miss his companionship until you join him some day. So go ahead and cry about your loss. It will bring you quickly to Stage Five.

Case Study: Mrs. T. was a beautiful young wife who along with her husband was in full-time Christian work. But depression and anxiety following her father's death prevented her from serving God very effectively for two years. Her father had himself been severely depressed and committed suicide. Mrs. T. came from a stoic religious background which discouraged crying when someone died. She had never really grieved over the loss of her father, whom she loved dearly. With the use of a Gestalt technique she pretended her father was sitting in an empty chair and told him how much she missed him and anything else that was on her mind. She also hesitated at first, then poured her heart out. She cried as never before. When psychological testing was repeated a few weeks later, her depression had declined significantly.

Stage 5: Resolution

Stage 5 is a rather brief stage which occurs once a person has worked through his denial, anger turned outward, anger turned inward, and genuine grief (weeping). During resolution he regains his zest for life and joy. Resolution occurs automatically after stages one through four.

Every normal human being, after suffering a significant loss or reversal, goes through all five stages of grief. The entire process in a mature individual will take from three to six weeks after a very significant loss such as the death of a mate. But knowing the dynamics of all five stages does not prevent grief reactions from occurring after a significant loss—it simply helps the individual speed through the five stages somewhat more rapidly and with less fear. *Every human will suffer temporary grief reactions* from time to time, but if a person puts into practice the knowledge he gains from this book, *there is no reason why he should ever get clinically depressed*. *Happiness*, in the long run, *will be his choice*. *Happiness is a choice!*

PART TWO

What Causes Depression?

5

Is Genetics a Good Excuse?

As physicians who have researched genetics quite thoroughly, we get disgusted with people who blame everything on their "bad genes"! People today are actually blaming such sins as alcoholism and homosexuality on "bad genes." The so-called scientists who do such things are slanting the data and grasping for straws.

Our genetic make-up does have an enormous effect on our intellectual and emotional potentials, but our degree of wisdom and happiness as adults is *not predetermined genetically* (as some would like to think). Most human depression is the result of our own irresponsible behavior—our own irresponsible handling of our anger and guilt. Some individuals are irresponsible because they choose to be, but others are irresponsible because of lack of knowledge. It is our hope that many readers of this book will grow in knowledge of how to handle their own emotions responsibly and put that knowledge into action.

Most human beings, however, hate to face up to their own human responsibility, especially when it comes to their own emotional state. It is so much easier to blame all our woes on bad parents, a poor mate, unfair treatment by the world, hypoglycemia, or—in today's modern world—"bad genes."

Our genes can predispose us to getting drunk more readily than someone else, but our genes don't magically get us to drink alcohol. Our genes may give some males fewer androgens than others, but our genes don't force anyone to engage in homosexual behavior. No one is genetically programmed to become a homosexual. That is purely a myth! Our *genes can predispose* some people toward developing a clinical depression under stress because of a depletion of norepinephrine in the brain (whereas someone else might be predisposed toward schizophrenia under similar stresses because of an alteration in the level of dopamine in the brain), but our genes do not force us to hold grudges against ourselves or others. The irresponsible action of holding grudges is what brings on the majority of depressions.

As Christian psychiatrists, we believe that the genetic potentials and predispositions of each individual are in the plan of God. God allowed each of us to have certain strengths and weaknesses as part of His plan to ultimately bring glory to Himself. In Psalm 139:13, 14, the psalmist David prays, "For Thou didst form my inward parts; Thou didst weave me in my mother's womb. I will give thanks to Thee, for I am fearfully and wonderfully made." In Isaiah 43:7, God says, "For I have created him for my glory, I have formed him; yea, I have made him." Why God didn't make any of us humans perfect we don't know, but we trust the God of all wisdom, love, and justice to make the correct ultimate decisions. To be angry at God for not being more "humane" is naive, arrogant, and pompous. In our practice we run into many immature individuals who naively think they are wiser and kinder than God. They think God makes mistakes. But man looks at the pain of a moment, while God looks at the joys of an eternity. Man is capable of empathizing with the pain of depression. God not only empathizes with man's pain (Christ suffered the painful death of the cross), but rejoices in the growth toward maturity that is occurring in the individual who is responsibly working his way out of a depression.

At this point, some readers may choose to skip on to the next chapter. But for those who are somewhat more academically inclined, we have summarized some of the genetic data on depression below:[1]

1. The scientific studies done so far indicate that women are clearly more prone to depression than men. This predisposition is felt to be carried in the genes, although cultural factors must also be taken into consideration.

2. Research reveals that relatives of depressed individuals have a significantly higher incidence of depression than do individuals in the general population. In fact, with respect to all affective disorders the risk estimate for first degree relatives (parents, siblings, and offspring) exceeds that for the general population.

3. Studies of twins have influenced many scientists to accept the theory of a genetic predisposition toward depression in some individuals. In a study of thirty-eight pairs of twins, the concordance rate (that is, tendency for the second twin to become depressed if the first one is) was found to be 57 percent in monozygotic (identical) twins but only 29 percent in dizygotic (fraternal) twins. The genetic sameness of monozygotic twins could easily explain the difference, although cultural factors (e.g., a lower sense of identity) must also be considered. Another study of depression in twins showed a concordance rate of 67 percent in monozygotic twins reared apart and a similar but higher concordance rate of 76 percent in twins reared together.

4. The mode of transmission (dominant vs. recessive gene; autosome vs. sex-linked chromosome; single gene vs. multiple genes) is presently under much investigation. Some studies indicate that a gene on the short arm of the X-chromosome may

be responsible for predisposing some individuals toward depression (manic-depressive type).

5. Manic-depressive illness is a relatively infrequent disorder which, in contrast to most depressions, is considered largely genetic. It is marked by very severe swings of mood from a delusional, grandiose elation (usually with rapid, incessant speech) to severe depression with suicidal ideation. These swings of mood at times seem to be unrelated to environmental stresses. Thus, genetics is considered an important factor in manic-depressive illness. The manic phase is successfully treated with lithium salt, and the depressive phase with antidepressant medications. The concordance rate for parents of manic-depressive patients is 36 to 45 percent. The concordance rate for siblings of manic-depressive patients is 20 to 25 percent. However, the concordance rate for the incidence of manic-depressive illness in the identical twin of manic-depressive patients ranges in various studies from 66 to 96 percent.

The role of genetics as a primary cause of general depressions is greatly overemphasized in some circles. People overemphasize their "bad genes" to avoid facing up to their own behavioral and emotional irresponsibilities as the cause of their depression. On the other hand, counseling professionals should be aware of genetic predispositions toward depression. They should also become thoroughly familiar with manic-depressive illness, which is medically curable if diagnosed properly.

6

How Deep Do the Roots of Depression Run?

The roots of depression run deep.[1] A person who becomes clinically depressed for the first time at age forty in all likelihood had some contributing roots to his depression planted at age four. Some authors today (especially nonprofessionals) describe depression in very simplified fashion, as though the steps to depression were as simple as one, two, three. Any attempt to describe a single "depressive personality type," for example, is naive and erroneous. Psychiatric research describes at least ten major personality types with hundreds of combinations of various personality types or behavior patterns. All types of personalities get depressed from time to time, even though there are a few types which are particularly prone to depressions.

The human brain is much like a computer. In his earlier book (*Christian Child-Rearing and Personality Development*, Baker Book House, 1977), Dr. Meier summarized several hundred research articles on personality development to demonstrate that approximately 85 percent of our adult behavior patterns are firmly entrenched by our sixth birthday. In those crucial first six years of life, we copied our parents' behavior patterns, especially the parent of the same sex. We learned to automatically do what they did. If they repressed their anger, we too have a tendency to repress our anger. If they used physical illnesses or depression to gain sympathy, then, in all likelihood, we do too. Our parents also consciously or subconsciously rewarded and punished various behavior patterns during those crucial six years. They attempted to mold us according to their ideals, frequently with good motives but poor techniques. Most two- and three-year-olds, for example, are very much in touch with their angry feelings. When they feel angry, they know it and they express it, sometimes in appropriate and sometimes in inappropriate ways. When our children feel angry toward us, we encourage them to share their angry feelings in a respectful way. In fact, we thank them for doing so. If they show their anger by kicking, however, we spank them. However, many parents discourage their young children from sharing their angry feelings, even appropriately. In fact some parents punish their children for sharing normal angry feelings appropriately.

Do you remember as a child ever telling your father, "Daddy, I'm really mad at you right now. Could we talk about it?" Many of you probably learned to fear your anger instead, because being aware of and sharing your anger resulted in rejection or punishment. You then learned to deceive yourself into thinking you weren't really angry at all. You learned to repress your anger and displace it by kicking the dog or fighting with your siblings.

Thirty-five years later you get passed over for a promotion that you deserve. You experience normal angry feelings but aren't aware of them because you learned to repress such feelings at age three. You hold in unconscious grudges against your superiors several nights in a row. Serotonin and norepinephrine gradually become depleted from your brain amine supplies, and you develop insomnia, fatigue, loss of appetite, and many of the other physiological concomitants of depression. You tell all this to your family physician and he tells you that you are depressed and have pent-up anger. Even though he is absolutely right, you think he doesn't know what he is talking about. "Me? Angry? Why, I haven't been angry since I was three years old!" When he refers you to a psychiatrist, you get very angry, but you call this anger "frustration." You pay your physician well to tell you that you have hypoglycemia or a thyroid problem, but instead he disgraces you by insinuating that you might actually be depressed! How dare he!

A month later you have become progressively worse. You have seen three specialists who can't find anything wrong with you so you assume that all physicians are incompetent. Finally, you find some incompetent quack nutritionist or exorcist who tells you what you want to hear. You feel relieved for a few days, but the symptoms remain. By now you are suicidal and don't know why. Since like most people you avoid facing up to your own responsibility for your feelings, you assume it must be your mate's fault and you consider a divorce—a "solution" all too prevalent in present-day America.

As a last resort, you swallow your middle-class pride (upper-class people love to see psychiatrists) and see a psychiatrist. He gives you an antidepressant and weekly psychotherapy. He gets you in touch with your anger; he gets you to verbalize it and resolve it. Three to six months later you get off the antidepressants and feel great even without them. You have learned how to be aware of and how to handle your own anger—something you knew how to do when you were three, but your parents taught you to repress anger instead.

You may have grown up in a legalistic church that taught you that all anger is sin. Thousands are taught this and an astonishing number of Christians believe it. All this in spite of the fact that God's Word tells us to "*be angry* and sin not" (Ephesians 4:26). The Greek word translated "be angry" is actually a command (it was written in the imperative mood). That same verse goes on to warn us that *we should never let the sun go down on our wrath*! We should never hold a grudge past bedtime. If every Christian would obey this verse of Scripture, allowing himself to be angry but maturely getting rid of all grudges by bedtime, no Christian would ever get clinically depressed. Though Christ was without sin, He got very angry at times. He even whipped the "religious" moneychangers out of the temple because of His anger.

Of course, anger can be wrong and is often the result of immaturity. Perhaps more important than whether or not a person should be angry (when he is already angry) is how he handles the anger. This will be discussed in later chapters. As a person grows in Christ, the anger that comes on because of immaturity will become less and less frequent.

Many of us learned faulty ways of handling our emotions in the first six years of life, when most of our adult behavior patterns are learned. But God has given us a human will and His power to do all things (Philippians 4:13), including changing the erroneous "programming" in our computer-brains. The root problem in nearly all depressions is pent-up anger, either toward ourselves (true or false guilt) or toward others (holding grudges). These grudges are usually *unconscious* (that is, we are unaware of them), because we are ashamed or afraid to admit them to ourselves. In order to avoid the responsibility of dealing with our sin (the sin of holding grudges past sundown—sometimes for months or even years), we look for face-saving explanations for our depressive symptoms. Every few years, a new explanation becomes popular in our society and is generally accepted by a majority of people. Excuses commonly used in the past include endocrine disorders, hypoglycemia, nutritional allergies, inner-ear disorders, and (most recently) picking the wrong mate (in which case divorce was regarded as the remedy for depression). Without a doubt, *the roots of depression run deep*.

7

What Are the Primary Sources of Emotional Pain?

Even though pent-up anger is the root cause of nearly all clinical depressions, there are other painful emotions as well. The pain of loneliness, for example, can be quite severe, even though the lonely person may not be suffering from a clinical depression with all its symptoms. We believe there are three primary sources of emotional pain.

One of these primary sources is *lack of self-worth* (a low self-concept). Parents tend to place the heaviest demands on the oldest child, so the oldest child tends to be the most successful in terms of a career— and the least happy about it!

Any child from the oldest to the youngest can have a low self-concept, however. The youngest child, for example, is frequently smothered and overprotected. Hating to see her youngest child grow up and to let him go, the mother often allows him to become overly dependent on her. There is a tendency for this overprotected youngest child to become somewhat rebellious in his teens. He tries to conform to a peer group given to the abuse of alcohol or drugs. He allows them to think for him since he no longer wants his mother to do so, but is still afraid to think for himself. He develops a low self-concept because he feels inferior to the teen-agers he sees who are more independent than he is. To compensate, however, he ridicules those independent teen-agers to whom he feels inferior. His low self-concept is a painful burden to bear, and if this anger directed toward self becomes great enough, it can lead to a clinical depression. Depression can inflict persons of all ages—from a newborn who loses her mother to a 100-year-old who grieves his increasing debility.

Parents who are overly strict can also cause low self-concepts to be developed in their children. The child assumes the parents are correct and he blames himself for not being perfect. When he becomes a teen-ager or adult, this false guilt grows until his anger toward himself causes a clinical depression. This particular syndrome will be discussed in greater detail in the next chapter.

A child with a cold, rejecting mother and a passive or absent father will also have a low self-concept and be prone to depressions. As a little child, he frequently feels angry because his normal dependency needs are not met. An infant who receives too little physical stimulation, for example, will wither away and die, even if well fed—a syndrome known as marasmus or failure to thrive. This child will, in infancy, attempt but fail to achieve intimacy with his parents. Thwarted in this attempt, he will give up and withdraw. He develops a real fear of intimacy and sets himself up for repeated rejection by his peers later in life. Getting his peers to reject him is less painful than being aware of the fact that he is choosing to reject them because of his fear of intimacy developed in infancy and preschool years. An introvert with no friends has a low self-worth and is prone to depressions.

Alfred Adler coined the term *inferiority complex*. He and his followers have done a great deal to contribute to our understanding of its root causes. Lack of self-worth is definitely a major source of emotional pain in human beings.

A second major source of emotional pain in humans is *lack of intimacy with others*—or loneliness. No man is an island. We are designed by God in such a way that we need one another. Building intimate friendships is always going to have its occasional troubles along with its rewards. Humans are basically selfish and so even intimate friends will offend each other from time to time. But the pain from occasional conflicts with friends is far better than the constant, gnawing pain of loneliness. Loneliness, like depression, is a choice. The only people who suffer from loneliness are those who choose not to make the effort it takes (including the occasional rejections) to build a few close friendships. They allow their fear of intimacy to dominate their will, never realizing that they do *not* have to do so. Some individuals with this syndrome will compensate by becoming extroverts with many superficial friends, but no intimate friends with whom to share their deepest feelings. Some will compensate by becoming extremely obese, and then wonder why members of the opposite sex reject them. Many "loners" will imagine that other people do not want to get close to them. In reality, they are rejecting the intimacy of others. But in their imagination they blame others because they do not want to become aware of their own irresponsibility. This defense mechanism is known as *projection*, because they are "projecting" their own rejecting behavior onto others in much the same way that a slide projector projects the slide within *itself* onto a screen. Matthew 7:3-5 is an excellent description of projection and its hypocrisy.

Our need for one another's love is emphasized throughout Scripture. The apostle Paul, for example, encourages believers to "consider how to stimulate one another to love and good deeds, not forsaking our own assembling together, as is the habit of some, but *encouraging one another*" (Hebrews 10:24, 25).

Harry Stack Sullivan is a secular psychiatrist who has done extensive research and writing on interpersonal relationships and their dynamics. He has found that lack of intimacy with others is definitely a major source of emotional pain. Loneliness is not synonymous with depression, but loneliness certainly predisposes an individual to depression. The lonely person either accumulates grudges toward those he thinks reject him (though actually they do not), or else he accumulates grudges toward himself for being, in his own eyes, such a "reject." He may even have significant grudges toward God for allowing the death of a mate or of his only close friend. Any accumulated grudges contribute to the biochemical changes that set up a depression.

The third major source of emotional pain is *lack of intimacy with God*. We are convinced that deep within each human is a God-vacuum—an inner emptiness that can be filled only by a personal relationship with God through Jesus Christ. In Romans 1, Paul tells us that God uses even the beauty of nature to make mankind aware of his need for a relationship with the Creator. We have patients from every religious background imaginable, and yet, within two or three sessions, nearly every patient will bring up, in his own terminology, some spiritual problem he is dealing with, such as an awareness of his own sinful condition and a need for cleansing.

Dr. William P. Wilson, professor of psychiatry at Duke University, has done a great deal of research and writing concerning the benefits of an intimate relationship with God on our overall emotional health. Dr. Armand Nicholi, professor of psychiatry at Harvard, has also made major contributions in this area. Both Wilson and Nicholi are committed Christians.

In summary, the authors believe there are three major sources of emotional pain:

1. Lack of self-worth.
2. Lack of intimacy with others.
3. Lack of intimacy with God.

Any one of these sources of pain can predispose a person to accumulating grudges which may in turn lead to clinical depression. How to remedy the emotional pain fostered by these sources will be discussed in Part Three, "How Can One Overcome Depression?"

8

Do "Nice Guys" Finish Last?

Out of all the various personality types in our culture, there is one type that is more likely than any other to get depressed at some time in life. That type is the "nice guy" —the person who is self-sacrificing, overly conscientious, overdutiful, hard-working, and frequently quite religious. Psychiatrists call this type the obsessive-compulsive personality.[1] Most lay persons call him a perfectionist, or a "workaholic," or even a dedicated servant. Over 90 percent of the physicians and 75 percent of the ministers to whom we have given tests leaned primarily toward obsessive-compulsive personality traits. Lawyers, musicians, engineers, architects, dentists, computer programmers, and other professionals in general tend to have many obsessive-compulsive traits. That is probably why physicians, dentists, and musicians have the highest suicide rates. Missionaries frequently fall into this category as well.

Many find this surprising. It doesn't seem fair, does it? With all the lazy, selfish, good-for-nothing people in this world, it just doesn't seem fair that society's dedicated servants should be the most likely candidates for depressions and suicide.

But those who have made a study of the depth of unconscious human dynamics realize that it really is quite fair. They also realize that, to a large extent, depression is a choice. Suicide is a choice. And happiness is a choice. Those dedicated servants who get depressed have as many struggles with personal selfishness as the parasite on welfare, but the selfishness of the perfectionist is much more subtle. While he is out in society saving humanity at a work pace of eighty to a hundred hours a week, he is selfishly ignoring his wife and children. He is burying his emotions and working like a computerized robot. He helps mankind partially out of love and compassion, but mostly as an unconscious compensation for his insecurity, and as a means of fulfilling both his strong need for society's approval and his driving urge to be perfect. He is self-critical and deep within himself feels inferior. He feels like a nobody, and spends the bulk of his life working at a frantic pace to amass wealth, power, and prestige in order to prove to himself that he is really not (as he suspects deep within) a nobody. In his own eyes, and in the eyes of society, he is the epitome of human dedication. He is the medical researcher who spends seven days (and nights) a week in the lab in order to save mankind from various diseases while his wife suffers from loneliness and his sons become homosexuals and eventually commit suicide. He becomes angry when his wife and children place demands on him. He can't understand how they could have the nerve to call such an unselfish, dedicated servant a selfish husband and father. But he has such a strong selfish need to compensate for his inferiority feelings that he blinds himself to the truth. In reality, his wife and children are correct, and they are suffering severely because of his subtle selfishness. This is precisely the reason why so many of the children of pastors, missionaries, and doctors turn out to be rebellious.

Please don't misunderstand. Many pastors, missionaries and physicians really are godly men and women who spend time with their families and are very happy. We both work about fifty to sixty hours per week, but still manage to spend an hour or two nearly every night playing with our children, and both of us have intimate fellowship with our wives. It all depends on one's willingness to establish biblical priorities. The Bible says a man should not be a pastor unless he rules his family well and has children who are well-behaved. The pastor who can't say no to parishioners placing demands on him should not be a pastor. The pastor who devotes excessive hours to "the Lord's work" and neglects his family is really a selfish man who is building a bigger and better church for his own pride and selfish motives (though he is not usually aware of this).

And so it is that in their middle years, these dedicated servants, with a mixture of godly and selfish motives, become overwhelmed with anger toward God (for supposedly expecting so much of them), toward family and associates (for similar reasons), toward their children (for rebelling), and toward themselves (for not being perfect). They become severely, clinically depressed. In a weak moment, when they are suffering immense pain and hopelessness because of their lack of insight into the truth, they may even commit suicide. We hope and pray that the insights in this book will prevent such wastes of human potential. Legalistic perfectionism is so unnecessary. Depression is such a waste of valuable time. Suicide is so devastating to those who are left behind. Thank God that He can heal all wounds.

In this chapter we would like to share some valuable research findings on how perfectionism (obsessive-compulsiveness) is developed in childhood. Then we will discuss some of the dynamics which go on at an unconscious level in many perfectionistic workaholics. These human dynamics of the mind are difficult to explain in lay terminology, so the reader may need to study this chapter with extra care. We will conclude this chapter with a brief discussion of true guilt versus false guilt.

First of all, if you were an expectant mother and wanted to

experimentally produce an excessively perfectionistic child (God forbid!), the following information and instructions would be helpful.

According to the *Diagnostic and Statistical Manual of Mental Disorders* (DSM-II), obsessive-compulsive personality is the diagnosis for individuals who are "excessively rigid, over-inhibited, over-conscientious, over-dutiful, and unable to relax easily."[2] If this progresses to a neurosis, the condition is characterized by

> . . . the persistent intrusion of unwanted thoughts, urges, or actions that the patient is unable to stop. The thoughts may consist of single words or ideas, ruminations, or trains of thought often perceived by the patient as nonsensical. The actions vary from simple movements to complex rituals such as repeated handwashing. Anxiety and distress are often present either if the patient is prevented from completing his compulsive ritual or if he is concerned about being unable to control it himself.[3]

Here's how to produce an obsessive child:

1. Talk all the time, but don't be very active physically, and never listen to what your child has to say.
2. Expect perfect etiquette and manners from your child from his day of birth on. Don't tolerate any mistakes.
3. Be an introvert. Don't let him see you interacting in a healthy manner with other human beings.
4. Be very critical of the people around you—this includes your minister, your neighbors, your husband, and most importantly, your child.
5. Be a real snob.
6. Be sure to domineer your husband as well as your children. This is very important.
7. Emphasize morality as a way of being superior to other children, or of getting to heaven.
8. Don't make any serious commitments to God yourself, and be critical of the religious convictions of your child's grandparents.

9. Tell your child that his father is the boss, but in reality, allow your husband to be nothing but a figurehead.
10. Expect your child to be completely toilet-trained by the time he is twelve months old. Then, when he grows older, he can get even with you by being constipated much of the time.
11. Be a real miser with your money. Always save for the future, and don't let that future ever come.
12. Emphasize the letter of the law rather than the spirit of the law. Make your rules quite rigid, and never allow any exceptions.
13. Practice the Victorian ethic. Shame your child for being a sexual being.[4]

Research has shown that these are the kinds of principles the parents of obsessive children follow. This is quite consistent with my own feelings. Actually a degree of obsessiveness can be very beneficial in life. It can help a person to be hard-working, conscientious, and genuinely moral. Almost all of the physicians and medical students to whom we have given personality tests have several obsessive-compulsive traits. If they weren't organized and industrious, they would never make it through the grinding demands of medical school and private practice. And as was stated earlier, many seminary students and ministers are quite obsessive-compulsive also. This can help them to accomplish great tasks for God, provided they also know how to relax and enjoy life at the same time. I'm sure the apostle Paul had some healthy obsessive-compulsive tendencies, and he may have had to overcome some unhealthy ones. But obsessive-compulsiveness can get out of hand if we, as parents, use the thirteen rules listed above.

Let's assume now that you have followed all these instructions and produced an excessively insecure, perfectionistic child who is now married and graduating from college *magna cum laude*. Let's call him John P. Workaholic ("P." is for Perfectionism), and delve into the deepest levels of his unconscious thoughts. Let's take a close look at his unconscious dynamics now that he is an adult.

First, we notice that John P. Workaholic is *perfectionistic* in everything he does. He is overdutiful, overconscientious, and a *hard worker*. He is unable to relax. He is hard on himself and those that are close to him. Because he is so hard on himself and because his conscience is so strong, he is prone to become depressed. John has worked hard all his life, but is convinced that he has never done enough. He is *overly strict* and *overly rigid*.

John tends to exhaust all of his physical and mental reserves. John is financially successful, but even though he is successful, he is never satisfied because deep within he keeps demanding more and more of himself. John is very intellectual, but at the same time he often seems cold. *He tends to major in facts and not feelings*. Feelings are foreign to him. He is against feelings because feelings are harder to control than facts. John P. Workaholic has *an intense need to be in control of himself, his thoughts, and those he is around*. Because of this, again, he majors in facts; he engages in a great deal of intellectualization because he wants to avoid feelings. This pertains not only to uncomfortable feelings, but also to feelings of warmth, because they too are hard to control. John avoids feelings because he has many insecurities. In other words, by maintaining rigid control, he is able to keep in check many of the deep insecurities that he feels. Whenever he is no longer able to keep these insecurities in check, he becomes depressed.

John is a very obedient, submissive individual. But he is pulled by anger, and occasionally, his defiant anger will escape. He has an *obedience-defiance* conflict. When his *defiant anger* escapes, he develops an intense fear. This fear is in fact *a fear of authority*, and this fear drives him immediately back into obedience. This fear reminds him of his mother's rejection whenever as a child he became angry toward her. It is this fear that produces his traits of being dutiful, conscientious, and concerned. Thus, many of these traits that seem so good on the surface are often in reality motivated not from a healthy source, but from John's fear—his fear of parental rejection. His feelings of self-worth are based on his parents' conditional acceptance of him. John remembers early *childhood experiences when he was accepted on a conditional basis*. He was expected to live up to a performance standard, and, consequently, he thought that love was given as he attained a certain level of performance. This type of dynamic set John up to be an extreme perfectionist, to never be satisfied with himself, to *always be attacking himself from within*, and thus to be prone to severe depression.

As an adult John P. Workaholic feels insecure in his relationship to others, including God. Since the love he received from his parents was on a conditional basis, he usually sees God the same way. Thus he often has trouble with faith, and he *often doubts his salvation*. To counteract these doubts concerning his salvation, John takes an *extreme* Calvinistic viewpoint. He carries the sovereignty of God to an extreme, to the point that he believes the individual has absolutely no responsibility in regards to his salvation. Of course, the only human responsibility in regards to salvation is that one believe in Christ. However, John tends to carry the sovereignty of God even beyond this to the belief that there is absolutely no human responsibility. This helps John control his own deep-seated insecurities and fears that he might be rejected. In fact, however, John secretly asks the Lord into his life literally hundreds of times because deep within he does not feel God could possibly accept him on an unconditional basis. Thus, he *thinks* like a hyper-Calvinist, to relieve his guilt, but he *feels* like an Arminian—conditionally accepted.

John is critical of himself and his wife, and this constant critical nature affects them and their moods. From within, John is not only torn by this critical nature, but by intense anger. One has only to study John's mannerisms for a short time to realize how angry he really is. He reflects this in the expression on his face and in many of his movements, as well as in his rigid posture.

The time frame to which this compulsive individual usually relates is the *future*. John is ever striving and planning for future goals. He is never satisfied with the present. He is always committing more and more of himself. This is in contrast to John's wife, who has hysterical traits and is concerned more with present feelings. Whenever John gets more and more depressed, his thinking eventually shifts from the future to the past. He begins to worry a great deal over his past mistakes and failures.

There are several major defenses that John P. Workaholic uses to deceive himself. One of the major defenses is *isolation*, by which John isolates most of his emotions and feelings. He is seldom aware of his feelings. He even uses isolation during funerals. He will go through a funeral with an apparent calmness, but within he is being torn apart, and eventually this can cause depression. Another defense mechanism that John uses is called *undoing*. John has much guilt and is always trying to undo the things he has done wrong. He is usually unaware of this inner motivation to do many things which will undo his guilt. Another defense mechanism that John unconsciously uses is that of *reaction formation*. He guards against impulses and feelings by doing exactly the opposite of what he really would like to do. For example, John carries on his own private crusade against sexual promiscuity in order to counteract the strong sexual desires which he is repressing. These defenses serve to help John temporarily keep from becoming depressed. Suddenly to become aware of all his anger and fears and guilt and sinful desires would be overwhelming to John, so he deceives himself instead. What John really needs is Christian psychotherapy or discipleship so he can gradually gain insights and begin to change himself with the help of Christ. This is what sanctification is all about—dealing responsibly with the truth about ourselves through the power of God and the insights of close friends.

John P. Workaholic also has many unconscious rituals. The rituals help to control his anxieties, and are also used to avoid intimacy. Intimacy would arouse emotions, and his emotions are hard to control. John's church, like many others, is very ritualistic in its orientation, and this also helps John to avoid becoming close to others.

Three of John's chief concerns are time, dirt, and money. When John was a young child, time was an important issue. John was in a battle with his mother every time he went to bed and every time he went to the bathroom. These traits from early childhood were deeply entrenched and carried over to adulthood, so John P. is still very much concerned with time. He is also concerned with money because money brings him status and power. In John's mind, dirt becomes symbolic of the sinful desires and motives which he is unconsciously repressing, so John is very concerned with dirt. He is usually a very neat and clean person. He demands that his wife keep their house spotless. When feeling severely guilty, he washes his hands repeatedly to symbolically wash away his sins just as Pilate did at the trial of Christ. Unlike Pilate, however, John is thinking about something else and unaware of why he is performing this ritual.

John P. Workaholic feels insecure, powerless, and hopeless. He feels uncertain in an unpredictable world. Since he cannot control these insecurities, he develops an excessive need for control. John develops a false sense of omnipotence in order to control his own insecurities in an uncertain world. He behaves as though he were very confident, and frequently fools himself into thinking he is. He usually succeeds in fooling his associates anyway. John also has a strong urge *to intellectually know everything*. Again, he wants to be in utter control. In spite of his outward confidence, John often has a hard time making decisions because he might make a wrong choice, and he cannot stand being wrong.

He wants ultimate truth in all matters. This includes theological areas. When he doesn't see theological concerns in a clear-cut manner, depression results. When he has uncertainty, he uses rigid rules to control the uncertainty. His philosophical discussions of certain topics are frequently a way of avoiding responsibility. For example, if he can talk about what it means to be a good father and husband, he can avoid being one.

Even though John is usually a very punctual, orderly, tidy, and conscientious person, at times he will revert to exactly the opposite traits. For example, at times he will not be orderly, tidy, conscientious, or dutiful; rather than being on time, he will be late. As we stated previously, the perfectionistic traits are not derived from a healthy motivating force but from a fear of authority. The nonperfectionistic traits (untidiness, etc.) derive from his defiant anger and rage at having to be obedient.

John nearly always emphasizes facts over feelings. Indeed, he tries to feel with his mind. He attempts to talk to others at the level of theories in order to avoid emotions.

John is also very stubborn. He learned this trait at a very early age when he was obstinate concerning the wishes of his parents.

In summary, John P. Workaholic is driven intensely *from within*. In trying to control his anxieties, he develops many defenses; but as is the case with so many other obsessive-compulsive individuals, depression is the final outcome. He worries a great deal, and develops a clinical depression when his rigid life-style no longer sufficiently handles his intense drives from within.

If we studied John P. Workaholic's inner dynamics long enough, we would eventually see a majority of the following obsessive-compulsive traits. Some of these traits are beneficial and help him reach the top professionally. But other traits are pathological and result eventually in depression.

The obsessive-compulsive personality:

1. He is perfectionistic.
2. He is neat.
3. He is clean.
4. He is orderly.
5. He is dutiful.
6. He is conscientious.
7. He is meticulous.
8. The obsessive-compulsive individual does a good job.
9. But he works too hard.
10. And is unable to relax.
11. He is choleric.
12. He is overly conscientious.
13. He is overly concerned.
14. His conscience is overly strict.
15. His thinking is rigid.
16. He is inflexible.
17. He frequently rationalizes to deceive himself and defend himself.
18. He intellectualizes to avoid emotions.
19. The obsessive-compulsive is a good student.
20. He is well organized.

21. He is interested in facts not feelings.
22. He seems cold.
23. He seems stable.
24. He tends to split hairs.
25. He is anti-authority (at times).
26. He is pulled between obedience and defiance.
27. Obedience usually wins.
28. But occasionally defiance wins.
29. The obedience leads to rage.
30. The defiance leads to fear.
31. The fears lead to perfectionistic traits.
32. The rage leads to nonperfectionistic traits.
33. One basic problem is defiant anger.
34. The obsessive-compulsive person displays many opposite traits: conscientiousness—negligence; orderliness—untidiness.
35. He has three central concerns: Dirt (he is very clean); Time (he is punctual); Money (he wants a feeling of security).
36. He needs to be in control of self and others who are close to him.
37. He needs power.
38. He is intensely competitive.
39. He keeps his emotions a secret from others.
40. He feels with his mind (he is too logical).
41. One of his defenses is isolation of feelings.
42. Another defense is magical thinking (he thinks he has more power than he really does).
43. Another defense is reaction formation.
44. Another defense is undoing.
45. He struggles to engage others on the level of theories.

46. He is afraid of feelings of warmth (in early life they occurred in dependent relationships).
47. He postpones pleasure (unconscious guilt).
48. He lives in the future.
49. There is little variety in his sex life.
50. The obsessive-compulsive individual lacks spontaneity.
51. He is very insecure.
52. Theologically he takes an extreme Calvinistic position—he longs to control the uncertain world and avoid his own responsibilities.
53. He needs respect and security.
54. He craves dependent relationships.
55. But at the same time he fears dependent relationships.
56. He is very moral.
57. He has feelings of helplessness.
58. He needs to feel omnipotent.
59. He substitutes his feelings of omnipotence for true coping.
60. He has trouble with commitment.
61. He fears loss of control.
62. He focuses on irrelevant details.
63. He uses techniques to conceal his anger—he shakes hands frequently.
64. His handshake is rigid.
65. He has feelings of powerlessness.
66. He is extraordinarily self-willed.
67. He avoids recognition of his own fallibility.
68. He uses his defense mechanism to control aggressive impulses.
69. He avoids real conflicts by obsessive thinking (i.e., he dwells on a substitute obsessive thought).

70. The obsessive-compulsive personality is stubborn.
71. He is parsimonious (stingy with his love and time).
72. He is obstinate.
73. He is punctual.
74. He is frugal.
75. He is penurious.
76. He is disciplined.
77. He is persistent.
78. He is dependable in many ways.
79. He is reliable.
80. He has an overdeveloped superego.
81. He feels comfortable only when he knows everything.
82. He insists on ultimate truth in all matters.
83. He has exaggerated expectations of himself and others.
84. He appears strong, decisive, and affirmative, but is not; rather he is uncertain, uneasy, and wavering. He follows rigid rules to control his uncertainty.
85. He needs to appear perfect.
86. Theologically he doubts his own salvation.
87. The power of his own thoughts is exaggerated in his mind (omniscience of thought=parataxic thinking).
88. Words become a substitution for responsible action.
89. Much doubt is present because of the chance of being wrong. He fears being proven fallible.
90. He rechecks doorlatches to achieve certainty.
91. He is cautious in love relationships, because love results in concern about another's feelings which are not under his control.
92. Anger is expressed more easily than warmth because it encourages distance.
93. He has a single-minded style of thinking.

94. He is good at tasks that require intense concentration.
95. His parents were usually obsessive and demanded total devotion.
96. His parents gave minimal love.
97. As a child, he felt accepted on a conditional basis.
98. In his way of thinking everything is black or white.
99. He strives to accomplish superhuman achievements to overcome uncertainties in his world.
100. He despises indecisiveness in himself.
101. He has a tendency to respond to extremes.
102. In his view accepting one's limitations amounts to being average—and contemptible.
103. He has a grandiose view of himself.
104. The obsessive-compulsive personality is critical.
105. But he cannot stand criticism.
106. Rituals are important.
107. There are rituals in his religious system.
108. In his view commitment is tantamount to dependency and being out of control.
109. Marriage commitment is difficult. Co-existence is preferred.
110. He lives in the future.
111. He saves for a tomorrow that never arrives.
112. He discounts limitations of time.
113. He denies death.
114. His insistence on honesty in marriage results in telling all at times.
115. He has trouble admitting mistakes.
116. Courtship is sometimes characterized by excessive cautions or restraints.
117. He gives minimal commitment, but demands maximal commitment in relationships.

118. Each partner in the marriage pursues his own interests.
119. Intimacy is limited.
120. In marriage he is careful to do only his minimal share.
121. In marriage, he needs to do most of the thinking for his mate.
122. Sex is unspontaneous and routine.
123. Female perfectionists have difficulty with orgasm.
124. Male perfectionists sometimes have difficulty with premature ejaculation. This is a result of anxiety, which is related to his fear of loss of control.
125. If obsessive defense mechanisms do not work, the result is depression.
126. Theologically, he stresses minor doctrinal issues.
127. He likes lists.
128. He is legalistic in dealing with himself and others.
129. He is a chronic worrier.
130. The three P's of the obsessive: he is
    a. Pecuniary.
    b. Parsimonious.
    c. Pedantic.

It is fitting to conclude this chapter with a brief discussion of guilt. Guilt is a common cause of depression because guilt is a form of pent-up anger. Guilt is anger toward yourself. Just like anyone else, perfectionists have true guilt when they sin, but in addition to that they have an excessive amount of *false guilt* (feeling guilty for something that in reality does not violate any of the laws of God). There is a crucial distinction between true guilt and false guilt.

Freud seemed to think that all guilt is false guilt—that guilt itself is a bad thing. Most of the psychiatrists we have studied under and worked with agreed with the Freudian view that guilt is always an unhealthy thing. We disagree strongly. True guilt, in our opinion, is the uncomfortable inner awareness that one has violated a moral law of God. It is produced partially by the conviction of God's Holy Spirit, and partially by our own conscience. Our conscience is what Freud called the superego. Our conscience is molded by many influences in our environment, such as what our parents taught was right or wrong, what our parents practiced as being right or wrong (which isn't always the same as what they taught), what our church taught was right or wrong, what the people in our church practiced as being right or wrong, what our friends thought was right or wrong, what our teachers thought was right or wrong. If we studied the Bible, our conscience was also molded by what the Bible says is right or wrong, but even that is understood in terms of our own interpretations and sometimes misinterpretations. No two consciences are exactly alike. God's Holy Spirit is always right, but our consciences are frequently wrong. Someone with an immature conscience can do something wrong and not know that it is wrong; in that case his conscience will not bother him. By way of contrast, someone who has been taught that everything is sin may have an overgrown conscience. In that case his conscience will bother him even when he does things that God Himself does not consider wrong. This is what we call false guilt: feeling guilty for something that God and His Word in no way condemn.

True guilt is valuable. God uses it to influence us to change our minds about what we are doing. That's what repentance is all about. Then when we do what is right, instead of what is wrong, we will be in fellowship with God, and we will like ourselves more too. Doing what is wrong lowers our self-worth. Doing what is right greatly improves our self-worth. In our experience as psychiatrists, when people have told us they feel guilty, it has usually been true guilt. They feel guilty because they *are* guilty. And straightening out the wrong they were doing is sometimes all that is needed to straighten out their feelings of depression. But we have also had many Christians come to us, especially from the legalistic churches, to express feelings of guilt for things that the Bible in no way condemns. They may feel guilty for being tempted, for example. It's no sin to be tempted. But it is a sin to dwell on that temptation and yield to it. Christ Himself was tempted: "For we have not an high priest which cannot be touched with the feeling of our infirmities; but was in all points tempted like as we are, yet without sin" (Hebrews 4:15).

The apostle Paul talked about Christians who believed it a sin to eat meat that had been offered to idols (see I Corinthians 8). Back in Paul's day, the people would bring sacrifices to the pagan temples. Then the priests would cut up the meat and sell it to gain some spending money. They would sell this meat at a discount, compared to meat prices at the nearby butcher store. In some towns Paul preached in, the Christians thought it was immoral to buy that meat, since it had been offered to idols. It is understandable why they would think that; they are to be admired for wanting to do what they thought was right. Christians in other towns, however, thought it was perfectly fine to buy meat that had been offered to idols. It was much cheaper, and they could invest their money in better ways than to waste it on the expensive meat at the butcher shop. The apostle Paul said that God Himself had revealed to him that eating meat that had been offered to idols was all right. God told him there was nothing immoral about it in His eyes. But He cautioned Paul not to show off his liberty in front of Christians with weaker consciences (weaker in the sense of being more easily offended). So whenever Paul was in a town where Christians thought it was wrong, he wouldn't eat meat which had been offered to idols. That was diplomacy, not hypocrisy, and Paul undoubtedly did it out of love and empathy. He had more important things to teach, and he didn't want to hurt his testimony. Offending some of his audience by eating meat offered to idols would diminish his effectiveness. He knew that when people decide something is wrong, not even a direct message from God can change their minds!

Paul Tournier, a Christian physician from Switzerland, calls true guilt "value guilt," and he calls false guilt "functional guilt." Tournier says:

> A feeling of "functional guilt" is one which results from social suggestion, fear of taboos or of losing the love of others. A feeling of "value guilt" is the genuine consciousness of having betrayed an authentic standard; it is a free judgment of the self by the self. On this assumption, there is a complete opposition between these two guilt-producing mechanisms, the one act-

> ing by social suggestion, the other by moral conviction. . . . "False guilt" is that which comes as a result of the judgments and suggestions of men. "True guilt" is that which results from divine judgment. . . . Therefore real guilt is often something quite different from that which constantly weights us down, because of our fear of social judgment and the disapproval of men. We become independent of them in proportion as we depend on God.[5]

Dr. O. Quentin Hyder traces the roots of false guilt back to childhood:

> The causes of false guilt stem back to childhood upbringing. Too rigid a superego or conscience can only be developed by too rigid expectations or standards imposed by parents. For example, parents who excessively blame, condemn, judge, and accuse their children when they fail to match up to their expectations cause them to grow up with a warped idea of what appropriate standards are. Unforgiving parents who punish excessively increase guilt. Adequate and proper punishment given in love and with explanation removes guilt. Some parents give too little encouragement, praise, thanks, congratulations, or appreciation. Instead they are never satisfied. However well the child performs in any area of school, play, sports, or social behavior, the parents make him feel they are dissatisfied because he did not do even better. The child sees himself as a constant failure, and he is made to feel guilty because he failed. He does not realize at his young age what harm his parents are doing to his future feelings of self worth. He grows up convinced that anything short of perfection is failure. However hard he tries, and even if he actually performs to the maximum that he is capable of, he grows up feeling guilty and inferior.
>
> As an adult he suffers from neurotic or false guilt, low self-esteem, insecurity, and a self-depreciatory pessimistic outlook on all his endeavors and ambitions. He then blames himself and this leads to anger turned inward. He attempts to inflict punishment upon himself because of his feelings of unworthiness. His failures deserve to be judged and punished, and since no one else can do it for him, he punishes himself. This intropunitive retribution, part anger and part hostility, leads inevitably to depression. It can also cause psychosomatic complaints and inappropriate sorts of actions.[6]

Hyder says the only treatment for false guilt is understanding it and evaluating it for what it really is. Feelings of bitterness and pride need to be separated from what the patient interprets as guilt. The patient needs to understand that he has no right to condemn himself—only God has that right, and Christians should leave judging and condemning to God alone. Then he needs to set new goals for himself that are realistically attainable, and no longer compare himself to others who are more gifted than he is in specific areas. Instead, he should compare his performance with what he believes God expects of him. God doesn't expect us or our children to achieve sinless perfection in this life. But He does want us to seek His will in our lives to the best of our abilities.

The apostle Paul compares entering the Christian life to entering the Sabbath Day rest (see Hebrews 4:1-9). God wants us to rest in Him, and in His power. Martin Luther struggled for years with the legalistic expectations of his religion, until he clearly understood that "the just shall live by faith" (Romans 1:17), and that "man is justified by faith without the deeds of the law" (Romans 3:28). Then he began to trust God's grace rather than his own good works to save him. In 1529, Luther penned the famous hymn, "A Mighty Fortress Is Our God." In this hymn, Luther expresses his appreciation of the fact that our God is an all-powerful God and that we should let Him win our battles for us, resting in His power rather than our own. In the second verse of that hymn, Luther refers to God by the Old Testament name, Lord Sabaoth, which in Hebrew means "Lord of Hosts" and suggests God's omnipotence. Let's take a look at that second verse:

Did we in our own strength confide,
Our striving would be losing;
Were not the right Man on our side,
The Man of God's own choosing.
Dost ask who that may be?
Christ Jesus, it is He;
Lord Sabaoth His name,
From age to age the same,
And He must win the battle.

Some Christians have the notion that God is a mean old man, holding a whip and just waiting to crack us with that whip whenever we break one of His rigid rules. But the God of the Bible is not like that at all. God is perfect love, and perfect justice. God didn't make rules so He could whip us when we break one. God gave us principles to live by so we can enjoy the abundant life and the fruits of the Spirit. God has set up laws for human nature just as for physical nature. If we do not abide by God's principles, we will suffer the natural consequences He has established. Sin is the transgression of those laws or principles which God has set up (see I John 3:4). All of us have sinned many times. Paul tells us that "all have sinned, and come short of the glory of God" (Romans 3:23). He tells us that the ultimate reward for those sins is eternal death in hell, but that in perfect love and grace, God offers us the free gift of eternal life and forgiveness for all of our sins—past, present, and future (see John 1:12; 3:16; Romans 6:23; 10:13; Ephesians 2:8, 9).

When a person becomes a Christian, he is a new creation. Paul tells us that "if any man be in Christ, he is a new creature: old things are passed away; behold, all things are become new" (II Corinthians 5:17). But this does not mean he has reached sinless perfection. Far from it. Sanctification, which is the process of gradually becoming more and more like Christ, now takes place in the growing Christian's life. Just as a newborn babe needs milk, the newly reborn spiritual babe—the new Christian—needs a lot of spiritual milk. The apostle Peter said, "As newborn babes, desire the sincere milk of the word, that ye may grow thereby" (I Peter 2:2). The "word" means God's Word, of course—the Bible. Daily devotions are a must for continued growth in spiritual and emotional maturity. There's no reason why children can't start to read the Bible at an early age. Consider using an illustrated Bible story book for a two-year-old, and teaching short Bible verses to a four-year-old. Recall the time Christ's disciples were getting ready to chase some children away so He wouldn't have to bother with them. Christ told His disciples, "Suffer the little children to come unto me, and forbid them not: for of such is the kingdom of God" (Mark 10:14). Then Christ explained to His disciples that to become a part of God's kingdom even adults have to accept Him with the simple faith of a little child. Thus, we can be assured that God desires to be in communion with our children, and that their meditations on God and His Word will help them overcome temptations. Devotions are especially important during those four traumatic years between twelve and sixteen, when boys and girls grow into men and women, with all the associated hormone changes, impulses, cravings, and feelings of guilt and inadequacy.

The apostle Paul said, "There hath no temptation taken you but such as is common to man: but God is faithful, who will not suffer you to be tempted above that ye are able; but will with the temptation also make a way to escape, that ye may be able to bear it" (I Corinthians 10:13). This verse can be a tremendous help to the young teen-ager. Paul also said, "And my God shall supply all your needs according to His riches in glory in Christ Jesus" (Philippians 4:19, NASB). The human body, soul, and spirit have a multitude of needs. Satan will usually tempt us through our natural physical and emotional needs. These needs include air, food, water, stimulation, sex, love, self-worth, power, aggression, comfort, security, and relief from psychic tensions. Many Christians have been erroneously taught that living the Christian life means totally denying many of these natural needs. The Christian may be called upon by God to deny some of his wants, but God has already promised to supply all of our needs. There's a difference. No wonder so many people are afraid to become Christians. They have been told that becoming a Christian means denying many natural needs. What foolishness! God created these needs within us. He can use all of the needs in our lives for His own glory. He promises us in Philippians 4:19 that He will supply all our needs, not deny them. But He wants to supply them in His way, and according to His principles of love. Satan wants to supply these same needs in his way, according to his principles of selfishness, greed, and hate. Our needs are not temptations. Our natural human tendency is to meet our needs in Satan's ways. It takes the new birth and spiritual insights to see how we can meet these natural needs in God's ways, with much greater ultimate joy and satisfaction.

9

Can Depression Be Acted Out?

There is another personality type that is nearly opposite from the obsessive-compulsive (perfectionistic) type described in chapter 8. That personality type is known in psychiatric terminology as the hysterical personality.[1] Hysterical men and women are very emotional, extroverted, dramatic, impulsive, naive, and frequently seductive. They also tend to be good-looking and popular socially (especially among the opposite sex), and they possess a great deal of charisma. While the obsessive personality is somewhat more common in males, the hysterical personality traits are somewhat more common in females. Our culture tends to encourage this male/female distribution of personality traits.

Perfectionists *get* depressed the most, but hysterics *act* depressed the most. Hysterical females in particular frequently complain of depression. But careful examination seldom shows them to have the physiological concomitants—the symptoms of a true clinical depression—unless they have read a good book on depression lately. That's why we call these cases theatrical depressions. Hysterical individuals (both male and female), just like any other personality type, *do* get clinically depressed at times. But they have learned all their lives (since early childhood) either to fake depression or to put themselves into a temporary depression in order to manipulate people. They do this when they want attention, or to punish an authority figure (usually a parent, boyfriend, or mate) for not letting them have their own way.

When a perfectionist says that he (or she) feels seriously suicidal, we admit him to a hospital immediately for his own protection. But when a hysterical patient says she feels like committing suicide, our usual comment is, "Well, that's one option. What are some other ways you could show your husband that you are feeling angry toward him?" We discuss a few other options, such as *telling* her husband how she feels instead of *showing* him dramatically, and within a few minutes, her "suicidal depression" is resolved.

We have had scores of hysterical patients who have "attempted" suicide a number of times. One patient—a prostitute—"attempted" suicide seventeen times. But none of these patients have actually committed suicide, although some have come very close. We have read about situations where this type of patient has committed suicide, however. Usually it was accidental. For example, a hysterical female may be angry at her husband, so she overdoses on sleeping pills at 5:00 P.M., expecting him to be home promptly at 5:30 P.M. to rush her to the hospital emergency room. Instead the husband has a flat tire and gets home at 6:30 P.M. and finds her dead. She actually had no intention whatsoever of dying, but allowed her emotions to dictate her actions. Thus she impulsively, naively, and accidentally killed herself. We do take all suicide threats seriously, even from hysterical patients, because of the potential of accidental death. But we handle the suicide threats of hysterical patients matter-of-factly (not dramatically). In this way the hysterical patient is not rewarded for her threat, and also she can learn more responsible ways to express anger.

As is the case with the obsessive-compulsive personality, the roots of the hysterical personality reach back into childhood. If you were the mother of a female baby and (God forbid!) wanted to produce tomorrow's sex symbol (and hysterical personality), here are twelve easy rules you should follow:

1. Encourage her to always depend on you to make all her decisions for her so she won't have to learn how to think for herself.
2. Spoil her; always let her get her way, especially if she pouts or cries.
3. Never meet your husband's natural sexual needs. For warmth and affection he will become very close (too close, in fact) to his daughter instead.
4. Lie to yourself a lot, so she can learn to use the technique of denial for herself.
5. Always praise her for her looks, never for her character. Put a mirror on every wall, so she can continually admire herself. (This is one of the most important rules for producing hysteria.)
6. Whenever she runs away—and she'll probably do this frequently—be sure to run after her and apologize for not letting her have her own way in the first place.
7. Whenever she pretends to be sad and feigns a suicide attempt by swallowing a couple dozen aspirins or sleeping pills, be sure to save her dramatically and show her how guilty you feel for not letting her have her own way in the first place. This will be easy, since she will never overdose unless you or her boyfriend is nearby to rescue her. (Note: In the United States, less than one out of every twenty suicide attempts by females that get recorded end in actual death. In our experience, we have seen and talked to scores of females in emergency rooms after they have made a suicide gesture, and we have never yet seen one of them die from it, even though most of them claim they were really trying to die. There was even one woman

from up in the mountains who overdosed on four iron tablets after an argument with her husband! Twice as many men die of suicide. The reason for this is that men usually use guns or other violent means, and half of them die as a result of their attempt.)

8. Encourage her to become a movie star. By now she is so dramatic that acting would be quite natural for her.
9. Get divorced and remarried two or three times so she can learn what you already know: that all men are good-for-nothings, but you might as well live with one anyway.
10. Encourage her to wear the most seductive clothing. Actually, you won't need to encourage her much, because she will do this naturally to please her father, who keeps on praising her for her good looks rather than for her character. (Note: Over one-third of the hysterical females we have treated have had sexual intercourse with their fathers or stepfathers. Usually they claim they were raped by their fathers, denying the obvious fact that they also had a strong hand in the situation by seducing them, either consciously or unconsciously [of course, this in no way diminishes the responsibility of the father or stepfather]. Five percent of American women and 2 percent of American men have experienced incest while growing up.)
11. When she comes home from a date two hours late, you and your husband should scold her for such behavior. Then with a curious smirk on your face ask her for all the titillating details and do enjoy every minute of it. But try not to be aware of how much you are enjoying her adventure, even though she can tell that you are.
12. Reward her whenever she plays sick. Then she will learn to become ill rather than face up to her emotional conflicts, running from physician to physician but never finding out what's wrong, and getting angrier and angrier at those male chauvinist M.D.'s. (She continues to spend hundreds of dollars getting their advice, however.)

According to the *Psychiatric Diagnostic Manual,* which is the bible of psychiatry throughout the world, individuals with hysterical personality disorders are "characterized by excitability, emotional instability, over-reactivity, and self-dramatization.

This self-dramatization is always attention-getting and often seductive, whether or not the patient is aware of its purpose. These personalities are also immature, self-centered, often vain, and usually dependent on others." Hysterics also have a higher than normal incidence of what we call passive-aggressive personality traits, which include "obstructionism, pouting, procrastination, intentional inefficiency, or stubbornness." These are ways of getting even with the person they are dependent upon without being openly hostile. Lest we become overly introspective, most of us have behaved in some of these ways some of the time, but individuals with true hysterical personalities behave in almost all of these ways almost all of the time. It's a matter of degrees.

At this point we present two brief case studies—a female hysteric who underwent treatment for several years, and a male hysteric (a Roman Catholic priest) who was treated for a couple of months. We have already met Jane as an example of denying grief (p. 36). When she was fourteen, she was admitted to the psychiatric ward of a general hospital after repeatedly running away, some minor drug abuse, and some bizarre behavior patterns. For example, she cut up her back with a razor blade in the school bathroom, then ran into her classroom, telling her female teacher—whom she had a crush on—that her sister had cut her. Jane would do almost anything to get attention! When we saw her talking to the juice carts on the ward, we thought she must have been completely out of her mind, but we found out later that even this was a dramatic attention-getting device. After intensive psychotherapy for six weeks in the hospital, Jane had weekly outpatient psychotherapy sessions for two years. During that period Jane ran away once more for half a day, overdosed half a dozen times or so in attempts to manipulate her mother, smoked marijuana occasionally, and had about a hundred temper tantrums. All of this was a dramatic improvement over her previous behavior. When she was sixteen, she went to live in a youth home for girls; by this time she had matured quite a bit. When she was first a patient at age fourteen, she was operating at about the three-year-old level of psychological maturity, even though her I.Q. was tested out at 135. By the time she was sixteen years old, she was behaving very much like a ten-to-twelve-year-old most of the time.

Parents sometimes bring in a teen-ager whose rearing they have bungled for fourteen or sixteen years, and expect the psychiatrist—since he has that magical "Master of Deity" degree—to correct all their mistakes in a few weeks of therapy. It doesn't work that way! All we can do is help the parents to find some ways to modify the 5 or 10 percent of that teen-ager's personality that isn't already formed. In reviewing Jane's first six years of life, it was discovered that she was born into an upper-class family in which the mother was extremely Victorian and the father financially successful, but psychologically very weak and immature. The boss of the family was a very domineering maternal grandmother, who was also a business executive. Since Jane's father was immature, and Jane's mother never satisfied him sexually—thinking sex was somewhat vulgar—Jane's father turned all of his attention to Jane. He completely ignored his wife and the other children. He praised Jane over and over again for how cute she was, and wouldn't think of disciplining her for anything. Whatever Jane wanted, Jane got. Her father and mother slept in separate bedrooms, and Jane slept every night with her father. During her preschool years, Jane was molested at least once by her maternal grandfather, who was becoming somewhat senile and had never gotten sexual satisfaction from his domineering wife.

When Jane was five, she and her father were lying in bed together when, all of a sudden, her father had a heart attack. An ambulance was called, and as he was being carried out of the bedroom, he told his frightened daughter, "Don't worry, Honey, I'll be back." But he died at the hospital, and Jane refused to believe that he was dead. For months she would look for him in closets and behind doors. He was her whole life. With her vivid imagination, she would conjure him up several times a day and imagine him walking into her room to talk to her. She finally quit doing this when she was sixteen, though she may still be doing it on rare occasions. Using her strong denial technique, she would actually believe he was there sometimes.

In her childish way of understanding, Jane blamed her father for leaving her when she needed him so much. In reality, she probably would have been much worse if he had lived and continued to treat her the way he did—like a substitute wife. So she loved her father and hated him at the same time. She became bitter towards men in general, and more and more seductive as she grew older. She developed a very hysterical personality with all of its characteristics. Seeing her therapist regularly for over two years, she learned to trust and identify with an older male who would not yield to her seduction and manipulation, but who showed her genuine Christian love in a matter-of-fact way. During the course of therapy she did put her faith in Jesus Christ, and she tried off and on to grow in the Lord. But she found herself trying to manipulate God in the same way that she had manipulated her father. As most people do, she thought God must be a lot like her father, and had difficulty accepting His omniscience, omnipotence, omnipresence, and His divine mixture of genuine love and perfect justice.

An attempt was made to teach Jane's mother how to handle her at home. But her mother, who had arthritis and a heart condition, simply could not force herself to discipline Jane in the way she needed to be disciplined, so Jane went to live in a youth home for girls in a nearby city. At last report she was doing quite well there.

As stated earlier, not all hysterics are women. If you apply the same techniques we have listed to your son, you can just as easily make a male hysteric out of him, and there are quite a few male hysterics around. Some of you may know one. We hope none of you is married to one. Here is the case study of a male hysteric—a Roman Catholic priest. He complained about all of his superiors, who were constantly misinterpreting his actions. Whenever his superiors would walk into the church and find him caressing a female parishioner, they would accuse him of being overly seductive. Of course, in his view he was only showing her sympathy for her marital and other problems. He complained that his bishop kept harassing him because of his liberal ideas about women's liberation and other women's rights causes. Complete psychological testing, including the Rorschach ink-blot test, was ordered for him. It turned out he was a male hysteric who unconsciously hated women. When he saw a feminine ink blot, he would think it was an atomic bomb. It all stemmed back to his relationship with his neurotic mother, who pampered him all his life and continually praised him for his appearance rather than his character. She also followed most of the other steps listed above.

Hysterics traditionally seduce persons of the opposite sex, either consciously or subconsciously, so they can put them down and prove that they are good-for-nothings like everyone else of the opposite sex. Many prostitutes are hysterics. Many a female hysteric seeks a good man to bring down sexually, so she can tell everyone that he seduced her, thus ruining his reputation. Many of them even make up stories of ministers and physicians who supposedly have seduced them. The Book of Proverbs describes hysterical females and males better than any book on psychiatry we have read. Solomon describes the hysterical male: "A naughty person, a wicked man, walketh with a froward mouth. He winketh with his eyes, he speaketh with his feet, he teacheth with his fingers; Frowardness is in his heart, he deviseth mischief continually; he soweth discord" (Proverbs 6:12-14). Solomon calls hysterical females "strange women" and says that they seek out the precious life, to bring him down. He warns godly young men that:

> The lips of a strange woman drop as an honeycomb, and her mouth is smoother than oil: But her end is bitter as wormwood, sharp as a two-edged sword. Her feet go down to death; her steps take hold on hell. Lest thou shouldest ponder the path of life, her ways are moveable [unstable], that thou canst not know them. Hear me now therefore, O ye children, and depart not from the words of my mouth. Remove thy way far from her, and come not nigh the door of her house: Lest thou give thine honour unto others, and thy years unto the cruel: Lest strangers be filled with thy wealth; and thy labours be in the house of a stranger; And thou mourn at the last, when thy flesh and thy body are consumed [probably referring to the devastating effects of syphilis], And say, How have I hated instruction, and my heart despised reproof; And have not obeyed the voice of my teachers, nor inclined mine ear to them that instructed me! I was almost in all evil in the midst of the congregation and assembly. Drink waters out of thine own cistern, and running waters out of thine own well. Let thy fountains be dispersed abroad, and rivers of waters in the streets. Let them be only thine own, and not strangers' with thee. Let thy fountain be blessed: and rejoice with the wife of thy youth. Let her be as the loving hind and pleasant roe; let

> her breasts satisfy thee at all times; and be thou ravished always with her love. And why wilt thou, my son, be ravished with a strange woman, and embrace the bosom of a stranger? For the ways of man are before the eyes of the Lord, and he pondereth all his goings.
>
> —Proverbs 5:3-21

In order to gain an even more intensive understanding of the unconscious dynamics in the mind of an overly emotional (hysterical) adult female, let us take an imaginary trip into the innermost thoughts and emotional strivings of Marilyn S. S. Charisma ("S. S." stands for subtly sexy).

Marilyn S. S. Charisma is a sociable, well-liked adult female who is presently working on her second marriage. Her first marriage was at age seventeen. He was a Don Juan-type—charismatic, very handsome, but dependent. It was a matter of their having to get married, since she naively "overlooked" the fact that sex can lead to pregnancy. In reality, on an unconscious level she wanted to get pregnant in order to punish her father. She and her first husband had marital conflicts right from the start, and both were too irresponsible to work out their own personality conflicts through counseling, so they divorced each other and blamed it on "incompatible personalities." This is a common excuse. (In reality, there is no such thing as "incompatible personalities," just *unwilling* personalities. Any two personality types can, with God's help, some quality counseling, and some swallowing of pride, develop a happy marriage. But both partners must be willing to make some responsible changes.)

Marilyn could not stand being independent after the divorce, so she soon married a successful, older, logical, stable, confident professional. She did not understand that he was quite obsessive-compulsive and that his stability and confidence were only a facade. She also did not realize that he was, for her, a father substitute.

Now, as we take our imaginary journey into Marilyn Charisma's thought processes, we begin to see things more clearly. We see, for example, that Marilyn is *emotional* and excitable, and seems depressed at times. But at other times, she can be very likable and have a very *pleasant personality*. She can be extroverted and outgoing. She can be the life of a party; people tend to gather around her because of the excitement she radiates from her life. She really has charisma. People enjoy being with her. She is often theatrical. She is very attractive physically. We see that she particularly desires attention. She is vivacious. Her language is often dramatic and expressive. She is a charming individual and has the ability to put others at ease while she herself is not at ease deep within. While she is emotional on the surface, she has *trouble getting close to others on a deeper level*. She emphasizes feelings rather than logic.

Her time frame is the present rather than the future or the past. The time frame of her husband is more in the future, since he is planning and setting his future goals. Marilyn's social friends usually do not notice that she is quite vain and self-centered. Around males she *uses her good looks to get the attention she so desires*. *She substitutes physical closeness for emotional closeness*. She has occasional affairs with other men, especially when her husband is out of town. She doesn't enjoy sex very much, but loves male attention and uses sex to manipulate these other men into satisfying her need for attention. She feels inferior—like a nobody. She doesn't like the way she looks, even though she is beautiful. Through her sexual prowess and attention-getting ability she tries to prove to herself that she is not a nobody. When her husband does not spoil her, she takes an *overdose* of a few aspirin or valium. However, she does not take enough of the pills to kill herself—she takes just enough to manipulate her guilt-ridden husband. She is subtly seductive in both dress and actions, so she can gain the attention she desires. She has many dependency needs. She *intensely fears rejection*.

She has many *conflicts with the opposite sex*. She sometimes undervalues and at other times overvalues the opposite sex. She has many *conflicts with her father* (who was a very immature man) *that were never resolved*. She remembers having learned in childhood that she could control her father by her manipulative actions, but she also found that he was unpredictable at times. She felt rejected by him. This left her with a fear of being rejected by other men later in life and with an ambivalence toward men. Because of her strong pent-up anger toward her father and other men, she is sexually frigid with her husband, although she can to some extent enjoy sex with other men.

Socially, she conveys the impression of being very warm and charming, but her life is unstable because of her overemphasis on feelings and lack of logic. Feelings are important, but since they are fickle and changeable she also is fickle and changeable at times. Marilyn S. S. Charisma represses many of her deep emotions, while seeming quite emotional on the surface. She seems very open, and new acquaintances feel they have known her for a long time. However, she has difficulty establishing more than just a surface relationship with anyone. In other words, acquaintances *know her no better after several months than after having known her for one hour*. Marilyn creates an outward impression of poise and self-confidence, but inwardly, she feels insecure. Boredom is a problem Marilyn faces often. Marilyn's husband is always punctual, but she is usually late. She does this unconsciously to punish her husband. He plans everything in detail, but she is not concerned with details. Her husband is extremely disciplined, but Marilyn is very impulsive and relies on impressions and quick hunches. She is very creative both in art and music, and has a vivid imagination. Her husband is very strict with money, but Marilyn is very extravagant.

Marilyn S. S. Charisma also has a hostile need to compete with men and a desire to achieve power over men through sexual conquest. Through sex, she can attract and control men. She chooses men who are all-powerful father figures. They see her as a status symbol because of her looks. She also is somewhat of a mother figure, which satisfies their dependency needs.

The fantasies of Marilyn Charisma tend to center around love and attention, while those of her obsessive-compulsive counterparts center around acquiring power. As a child, Marilyn learned that she could receive increased attention by being sick. Also as a child she learned that dramatic scenes helped her to obtain her way. She learned to be overly dependent on her mother, and this gave her difficulty in maturing. She felt, moreover, that special privileges were accorded to men; she reacted with competitive envy and developed what is known as castrating behavior. She was very close to her father when she was very young, but conflicts developed, and she felt an extreme sense of rejection at the time of puberty. By her teen-age years, Marilyn became preoccupied with obtaining approval of others. She had poor relationships with other good-looking females because of the competition for the attention of males.

All of us have some hysterical personality traits. The more hysterical we are, the more of the following traits we have:

1. The hysterical individual is likable.
2. She has a good personality.
3. She is outgoing.
4. She is the life of the party.
5. She is fun to be with.
6. The hysterical personality is dramatic.
7. She is theatrical.
8. She is sanguine.
9. She is unstable.
10. She is emotional.
11. She is excitable.
12. She emphasizes the present.
13. She emphasizes *feelings*.
14. She is vain.
15. She is self-centered.
16. She is dependent.
17. She is naive.
18. She is manipulative.
19. She may overdose as a suicide gesture.
20. The hysterical individual is seductive in dress.
21. She is also seductive in action (usually in subtle ways of which she is not aware).

22. She is ambivalent toward the opposite sex.
23. She does not think enough (she relies too much on feelings).
24. Her logic is poor.
25. Her chief defense is denial.
26. Another defense is displacement (for example, displacement of her repressed anger toward her father unto other men in general).
27. The basic problem of the hysterical individual is an unconscious anger (hatred) toward the opposite sex, even though she craves their attention.
28. She is overreactive.
29. Her behavior is attention-seeking.
30. She is looking for a father figure.
31. But she hates that father figure.
32. There is a deep-seated bitterness toward her father.
33. She is immature.
34. She is charming.
35. She is vivacious.
36. Her language is expressive.
37. Her language has many superlatives.
38. Though able to put others at ease, at the same time she herself doesn't feel at ease.
39. She is outwardly warm.
40. She seems very open—she shares too much too quickly.
41. Others come to know her quickly and soon feel like old friends.
42. However, deeper intimacy seldom develops.
43. She has trouble developing real feelings of love and intimacy.
44. She constantly seeks love.
45. She is emotionally labile.

46. She has a good imagination.
47. The hysterical individual is attractive physically.
48. Her presence adds to her surroundings.
49. She is sensitive.
50. A listener finds himself drawn into her view of the world.
51. She exaggerates to dramatize a viewpoint.
52. She is verbally expressive.
53. She conveys an outward impression of poise.
54. She conveys an outward impression of self-confidence (but this confidence is false).
55. Her self-image is one of insecurity.
56. Her self-image is one of apprehension.
57. Boredom is a constant problem.
58. The hysterical individual is disorderly.
59. She is unconcerned about punctuality.
60. She has difficulty planning details.
61. Mundane tasks are burdensome.
62. She is impulsive.
63. She relies on quick hunches or impressions, not critical judgment or convictions.
64. She likes tasks that are exciting or inspiring.
65. She does not like routine work.
66. She is suggestible.
67. She can be easily hypnotized.
68. There is an aura of egocentricity about her.
69. She is concerned with her external appearance, her looks.
70. Her needs must be immediately gratified.
71. She is extravagant.
72. Hysterical individuals may experience disturbed sexual

functioning. A man may experience premature ejaculation. A woman rarely if ever has orgasms until her emotional conflicts are resolved through therapy.

73. A hysterical woman may experience partial frigidity. She does not like sex with her husband.
74. She fears her own sexual feelings.
75. She is hostile toward and competitive with other good-looking females.
76. She desires to achieve power over men.
77. She seeks conquest, through seduction.
78. She selects an all-powerful father figure.
79. But sometimes she selects a dependent person so she can control him.
80. She is a hypochondriac; she avoids facing her emotional problems by thinking she is physically ill.
81. Her fantasies center around receiving love and attention.
82. She has a rich fantasy life.
83. Her surface emotions defend against deep emotions.
84. She has fears of rejection.
85. She was the youngest female or had some other special position in her family.
86. Her mother was competitive, cold, resentful, jealous.
87. But her mother was warm when her child was sick or acted sick.
88. She was so overly dependent on her mother that she didn't mature.
89. She continuously relies on others for self-esteem.
90. She went through a prolonged tomboy stage as a teen-ager.
91. She competes directly with men.
92. Her father was charming and controlling.
93. Her father was sociopathic or alcoholic.
94. She was very close to her father in her youth (below age five).

95. Her father encouraged her emotional nature.
96. At puberty she felt rejected by her father.
97. Her girl friends were unattractive.
98. She attempts to avoid responsibility for her emotional responses.
99. She fears the adult life role.
100. She has a seductive handshake.
101. She experiences mood changes.
102. She wants to conquer the opposite sex.
103. She has trouble seeing the opposite sex realistically. She either idealizes a man or thinks he is worthless.
104. She is undisciplined.
105. Hysterical men compete for the attention of the women in the immediate environment.
106. Hysterical women compete for the attention of the men in the immediate environment.
107. Sexual conflicts are denied and transferred symbolically to imagined severe pain in the sexual organs or lower back.
108. Many hysterics undergo multiple surgeries as adults, especially on their sexual organs and lower back (after years of chiropractic massages).
109. Many female hysterics get their uterus removed before age forty because they unconsciously resent being women.
110. Theologically the hysterical individual leans toward Arminianism.
111. The religious leanings of the hysterical individual are toward emotional experiences rather than relying on God's Word.
112. She has many "spiritual" ups and downs.
113. She blames the devil for everything in order to deny her personal responsibility and guilt.
114. She is religiously grandiose at times, claiming special powers and gifts.

115. Even in church-related activities she unconsciously seeks attention.

116. She is frequently angry at God for not doing things her way.

117. She quits personal daily devotions whenever God doesn't do what she tells Him to. In this way she gets vengeance on God, but she has no idea that this is her real reason for quitting devotions.

118. The sinful temptations confronting hysteric personalities are predominantly in sexual areas, sometimes including homosexual temptations.

10

What Precipitating Stresses Bring On Depression?

But now thus says the LORD your creator,
O Jacob, and He who formed you,
O Israel: "Do not fear,
for I have redeemed you; I have called
you by name; you are Mine!
When you pass through the waters,
I will be with you;
and through the rivers,
they will not overflow you.
When you walk through the fire,
you will not be scorched,
nor will the flame burn you.
For I am the Lord your God,
the Holy One of Israel, your Savior"
(Isa. 43:1-3a).

The next time you feel sorry for yourself for having a financial setback, or an uncommunicative mate, or some other stress that seems to precipitate depressive feelings, think about the nation of Israel. Think about the horrendous stresses Israel has undergone throughout history; there are many lessons you can learn. Israel still exists today, and always will. God will also allow Christians to suffer whenever they wander away from His guidelines for a happy life. But Israel still stands, in spite of her sufferings. Neither will God allow His church—His children—to be destroyed. If we allow Him to, He will bring us through "precipitating stresses"—even when those stresses seem overwhelming. He will bring us through them even when they appear, from our perspective, to be insurmountable. These precipitating stresses can vary from finding out your child has leukemia to finding out that your mate is having an affair. They can include any situation that you, as an individual, perceive as acutely stressful. We bring most of these stresses upon ourselves, through either direct or unconscious irresponsibility. But it would be very naive and unwise to assume, as some Christians do, that *all* stresses are brought on because of personal sins and irresponsibility.

If a patient comes seeking advice and consolation because her child is dying of leukemia, we will genuinely grieve with her. We will help her to see that this is in no way the result of sin in her life, but that disease and death are as much a part of human life as are birth and falling in love. People erroneously assume that the death of their child must be punishment for some sin that they—the parents—have committed. To *assume* so is naive and self-centered. It is self-centered in the sense that we "self"-conscious humans tend to naively think that all of life's events somehow revolve around us, as though we were the center of the universe.

On the other hand, whenever a battered wife comes seeking advice and consolation because her husband beats her up twice a week, our usual response is, "Oh, really? How do you get him to do that?" In all the scores of cases of this nature that we have analyzed in depth, there was only one case in which the battered wife was not provoking (usually unconsciously) her explosive husband until he reached the boiling point (of course, this does not diminish the husband's responsibility). After a beating, the husband usually feels very guilty and spoils his wife for several weeks. In the meantime, she is getting from people around her the sympathy which she craves, and she is satisfying her unconscious needs to be a masochist. There is a variety of possible reasons behind her need to suffer. Perhaps she is seeking to relieve her own personal guilt or to prove that all men are beasts like her father. Most people marry someone very similar to their parent of the opposite sex, no matter how terrible that parent may have been.

This is just one example of what psychiatrists see day after day. We see humans who think they are in control of their lives but who are, in reality, allowing themselves to be dominated by their own unconscious drives, conflicts, and motives. The average person looks at the precipitating stresses in his environment that are making his life unbearable. But a wise counselor will try to look into that individual's heart—his unconscious thoughts and emotions—to see what that individual can do to quit bringing on his own precipitating stresses.

Again, look at the nation of Israel. How many of her stresses did Israel bring on herself—even though she was not aware that she was doing so? Why do you think wise King Solomon prayed for God to search his soul for secret sins? Why did wise King David pray the prayer: "Search me, O God, and know my heart; try me, and know my anxious thoughts; and see if there be any hurtful way in me, and lead me in the everlasting way" (Psalm 139:23,24)? What do you think God means when He continually refers to us humans as "people who are blind, even though they have eyes," and "deaf, even though they have ears" (Isaiah 43:8)? All of us humans have blind spots. We are the primary source of our own unhappiness. When we grow in God's wisdom and gain insights into our own self-deceit, then happiness is a choice. Jeremiah 17:9 is the key to Christian psychiatry: "The heart is deceitful above all things, and desperately wicked, who can know it?" The prophet Jeremiah is saying that we humans cannot fathom or comprehend how desperately sinful and deceitful our heart is—our unconscious motives, conflicts, drives, emotions, and thoughts. In Proverbs 8, Wisdom is personified. Wisdom calls out to all naive humans to listen and learn the path to success and happiness by replacing their ignorant human way of thinking with God's wise principles. Wisdom concludes (verses 35, 36) with the statement:

> For he who finds me finds life,
> And obtains favor from the LORD.
> But he who sins against me injures himself;
> All those who hate me love death.

Solomon said, "Where there is no guidance, the people fall, but in abundance of counselors there is victory" (Proverbs 11:14). Some people (especially in the lower middle-class) poke fun at getting professional counseling ("seeing a shrink"), but this ridicule is the product of their own naiveté and defensiveness. Getting guidance from a knowledgeable Christian pastor or professional counselor can help bring about victory over life's seemingly overwhelming stresses. To obtain and apply to one's life good-quality Christian psychotherapy is synonymous with discipleship. God sanctifies many people (brings them toward Christlikeness in their attitudes and behavior) through confrontation by loving and insightful friends, pastors, counselors—and even psychiatrists sometimes. Don't ever be ashamed to get counseling when going through life's stresses.

Scientific research indicates that 85 percent of significant depressions are precipitated by life stresses.[1] Scientific research further indicates that suicide attempts are usually preceded by acutely stressful situations in the person's environment. Following is a list of ten common precipitating stresses that are often found in cases of depression:

A Loss

Probably the most common stress that precipitates a depression is suffering a significant loss.[2] This loss may be the death of a loved one. In this case the feelings of sadness go beyond a normal grief reaction to a depressive reaction. The loss may be a divorce. A person loses his mate and his support system. Many of his dependency needs are no longer being met. The loss may even be a job promotion. A job promotion can be a real threat, because the individual may lose his excuse for not producing more, may feel inadequate in the new position, and thus may become very depressed. Maybe that is one reason why some individuals stay in graduate school so long—to avoid the threat of failure.

One character in the Bible that became very depressed partially as a result of the many losses he sustained was Job. Job lost his children and his estate. He lost essentially everything he had. He became very depressed. Later he overcame this depression with the Lord's help and again became very effective for the Lord.

Anger Turned Inward

Whenever we suffer a significant loss of any kind, we go through modified grief reaction (see chapter 4). We feel some anger, whether we are aware of it or not. If that anger is repressed, it will lead to depression. In other words, a significant loss *can* result in a depression if we handle our anger irresponsibly by not dealing with it. For example, a person may actually be angry at a loved one who has died. Nearly all children experience this and thus need counseling after the death of a parent or sibling to prevent a depression that can last for many years and can get worse each year on the anniversary of the loved one's death. Since it is unacceptable to express anger toward a dead person, the anger is turned on the self, and depression is the result. Over and over in the literature on the subject, depression is described as anger turned inward. In the vast majority of cases, anger is very apparent in the facial expressions, in the voice, and in the gestures of depressed individuals. They are often intensely angry, but usually they do not recognize their anger. They frequently get quite angry at psychiatrists who point out their problem with anger. They will vehemently deny their anger. If only they could see themselves on videotape, they would recognize their intense anger. They deny being defensive as well. Ways to deal with this anger will be discussed in a later chapter.

A Blow to the Self-Image

A blow to the self-image is often the precipitating event that is found in cases of depression.[3] Many divorced people become depressed because they feel rejected and their self-image has been hurt. This blow to the self-image can come from external circumstances that directly attack and lower one's self-concept. The blow to the self-image can also come from within. For example, whenever we sin, our conscience is bothered and our self-image is automatically lowered until that sin has been forgiven by God and by ourselves. Then our self-image is restored. It's amazing how many Christians will get involved in some sin for a few weeks or months and then wonder why they have become so depressed. When a patient tells us he has been depressed for two months, we frequently ask, "What have you been doing the past two months that might be causing your depression?" He will generally look surprised at the question, and then admit, "Well, I have been having an affair, but I didn't know that had anything to do with my depression." After confessing and forsaking his sin, and then forgiving himself as well, the depression goes away.

Adjustment Reactions

The term *adjustment reaction* is used to describe what happens to basically healthy individuals who are undergoing a situational stress and respond by becoming anxious or depressed to some degree.[4] In II Corinthians 4:8-10, the apostle Paul says, "We are troubled on every side, yet not distressed; we are perplexed, but not in despair; Persecuted, but not forsaken; cast down, but not destroyed; Always bearing about in the body the dying of the Lord Jesus, that the life also of Jesus might be made manifest in our body." All of us go through situational problems that at times make us feel anxious and depressed to a certain degree. However, we are usually able to cope with the problem and deal with it before it develops into a clinical depression.

False Guilt

As mentioned previously, obsessive-compulsive individuals are very hard on themselves, very critical of themselves.[5] They are prone to worry, and to false guilt. Eventually the worry and false guilt may overcome them, and the result is depression. In a sense, the person has turned against himself. The conscience is against the self in an unhealthy way, and the individual eventually gives in to the attack and becomes depressed. The Christians in Galatia were driven by an unhealthy guilt from within instead of being motivated by the love and grace of Christ. They were similar to many legalistic Christians who have false guilt and resulting depression today. Meditate on the Book of Galatians sometime soon if this is a problem with which you personally struggle.

True Guilt

True guilt can be a major cause of depression. True guilt with resulting depression is (and should be) the normal response in Christians who sin and do not turn to Christ. In fact, "Christians" who sin and do not have true guilt should question their salvation. Many godly men have suffered from depression because of sin and true guilt. King David stated, "When I kept silent about my sin, my body wasted away through my groaning all day long" (Psalm 32:3). In Titus, *seven* different groups of people are discussed; each group is characterized by certain personality traits. For example, the *elders* are to be blameless, not overbearing, not quick-tempered, not given to much wine, not violent, and so on. The older women are to be reverent, not slanderers, not addicted to much wine, and able to teach. Six of these seven groups of people share a common trait. In the King James version that trait is translated as being "sober." In the New American Standard version the word is translated "sensible." Perhaps the best translation of this word is given in the New International Version, which interprets the word as "self-controlled." It is very interesting that self-control is the only trait shared in common among the six groups. For the young men it is listed first. The lack of self-control, resulting sin, and then depression is the story of many Christians.

Take as a case in point a young lady who was living in adultery but felt no guilt or depression. She claimed to be a Christian. That worried us, and so we shared the following verses with her:

> Every one who practices sin also practices lawlessness; and sin is lawlessness. And you know that He appeared in order to

> take away sins; and in Him there is no sin. No one who abides in Him sins; no one who sins has seen Him or knows Him. Little children, let no one deceive you; the one who practices righteousness is righteous, just as He is righteous; the one who practices sin is of the devil; for the devil has sinned from the beginning. The Son of God appeared for this purpose, that He might destroy the works of the devil. No one who is born of God practices sin, because His seed abides in him; and he cannot sin, because he is born of God. By this the children of God and the children of the devil are obvious; any one who does not practice righteousness is not of God, nor the one who does not love his brother.
>
> I John 3:4-10 (NAS)

> But realize this, that in the last days difficult times will come. For men will be lovers of self, lovers of money, boastful, arrogant, revilers, disobedient to parents, ungrateful, unholy, unloving, irreconcilable, malicious gossips, without self-control, brutal, haters of good, treacherous, reckless, conceited, lovers of pleasure rather than lovers of God; holding to a form of godliness although they have denied its power; and avoid such men as these. For among them are those who enter into households and captivate weak women weighed down with sins, led on by various impulses, always learning and never able to come to the knowledge of the truth.
>
> II Timothy 3:1-7 (NAS)

These verses indicate that anyone who habitually chooses and willfully practices a known sin is not a Christian. The natural result of sin is guilt; and if that guilt is not resolved by confession to God, then depression results. Christians sin daily, and continually need to claim God's promise to forgive them their sins (see I John 1:9, which was written *only* for Christians). A true Christian will not be able to willfully continue in a known sin for a very long time without developing deep guilt and depression.

In Galatians 5:19-21, the apostle Paul informs us:

> Now the works of the flesh are manifest, which are these; Adultery, fornication, uncleanness, lasciviousness, idolatry, witchcraft, hatred, variance, emulations, wrath, strife, seditions, heresies, envyings, murders, drunkenness, revellings, and such like: of the which I tell you before, as I have also told you in time past, that they which do such things shall not inherit the kingdom of God.

These verses also indicate that a Christian cannot continue to practice sin. It should be pointed out that the key word is *practice*. The Christian does not practice sin. This is not to say that he never sins. We are also told in I John that we have all sinned. But the Christian does not make a practice of sin and living in sin. An individual does not become a Christian by professing to live a life of sinless perfection, nor does he become a Christian by making any kind of promise but rather by simply accepting what Christ has done for him. However, once a person does accept Christ, Christ's life within will not permit him to live a life of practicing sin.

Wrong Perspectives

A common precipitating cause of depression in many Christians is a wrong perspective. We live in an affluent society and in a society with many temptations. It is easy for Christians to get their eyes focused on the wrong perspectives. In Psalm 73:1-3 Asaph recorded the depression he suffered when he developed a wrong perspective:

> Truly God is good to Israel, even to such as are of a clean heart. But as for me, my feet were almost gone; my steps had well nigh slipped. For I was envious at the foolish when I saw the prosperity of the wicked.

In verses 16 and 17 of the same chapter, he finally got his perspective straight and his depression lifted.

> When I thought to know this, it was too painful for me; until I went into the sanctuary of God, then understood I their end.

Moses, on the other hand, had a more godly perspective. In Hebrews 11:24-26, we read:

> By faith Moses, when he was come to years, refused to be called the son of Pharaoh's daughter; Choosing rather to suffer affliction with the people of God, than to enjoy the pleasures of sin for a season; esteeming the reproach of Christ greater riches than the treasures in Egypt: for he had respect unto the recompence of the reward.

Because Moses had a godly perspective, he refused the pleasures of sin for he knew they would last but a season and would not give long-term meaning to his life. Many Christians with short-range perspectives will choose short-range behavior patterns such as taking drugs or having an affair in order to try to relieve the painful emotions they feel, but in the long run these behavior patterns only increase depression. These behavior patterns may give temporary relief, but only increase the pain over the long haul. On the contrary, an individual with a long-range perspective will choose behavior patterns that he will sometimes not feel like following, such as memorizing Scripture or studying the Bible daily, but in the long run, these behavior patterns will relieve painful emotions and enable the individual to feel good about himself.

A healthy perspective is to realize that only two tangible things will last forever—the Word of God and people. In Matthew 24:35, we read, "Heaven and earth shall pass away, but my words shall not pass away." In II Peter 3:10, we find that everything else will eventually be destroyed. A healthy perspective is to invest our lives in the only two things that have eternal significance—the Word of God and people. An unhealthy perspective is to let Satan trick us into investing our lives in things that are obtained through sinful means and that will not last, but give only temporary relief of emotional pain. A sound perspective is to spend our time raising healthy children and helping our family live godly lives. How often psychiatrists see the converse of this. For example, a middle-aged individual relates that he has decided to stop investing his time in his family and rather start investing his life in an affair. Of course, this gives only temporary relief and results in much more pain and many more emotional problems in the long run. King Solomon's conclusion after seeking fulfillment in sex, education, and pleasure was, "Vanity of vanities, all is vanity." We have been repeatedly impressed with individuals who lift their depression by getting their priorities straight.

Attacks by Satan

Another precipitating factor of depression is an attack by Satan. The apostle Peter stated that Satan walks about like a roaring lion seeking whom he may devour. The apostle Paul stated that we wrestle not against flesh and blood but against principalities, against powers, against the rulers of the darkness of this world, against spiritual wickedness in high places. Satan likes nothing better than to render Christians ineffective through depression. Christ desires that we confess our sins, solve our problems, and thus lift our depression.

When one is feeling down, how can he know whether God is trying to tell him something or whether he is just worrying? The following may be a helpful point. If the reason for the discouragement and depression is vague, in all probability this is not a special message from God, because God is not the author of confusion (see I Corinthians 14:33). Nor is it a special message from God if the individual feels totally helpless and sees no way out, for with God there is hope as one deals with the problem. Likewise, if the person feels downgraded and worthless, for with God one senses his worth and knows he can be built up through dealing with his problem.

Self-Effort

A major source of discouragement among dedicated Christians is trying to live and work for Christ in their own strength. Clearly, the Christian life is a super-natural life and can be lived only through the power of the Holy Spirit. Thus, the apostle Paul stated, "I can do all things through Christ . . ." (Philippians 4:13). In contrast, in Romans 7:24 he recorded the discouragement he experienced as a result of trying to live for God in his own energy.

If the Lord has a ministry He wants accomplished, and if an individual is available, God will accomplish what He desires. To be sure, assuming responsibilities (even in Christian activities) beyond what God desires is a major cause of discouragement.

Wrong Priorities

God is first of all concerned that an individual really gets to know Him (see Philippians 3:10). Secondly, God wants him to meet the needs of his family (see I Timothy 5:8). And thirdly, with the time left over after enjoying intimacy with God, mate, and children, God wants him to minister to others in the particular ways in which he is most able to be effective. Because of unconscious pride and strong needs for approval, many Christian workers neglect their family to "serve the Lord." Ignoring the need for adequate sleep and recreation is another wrong priority. Having wrong priorities is a major precipitating factor in most depressions. Proper priorities will be discussed more thoroughly in Part Three of this book.

In summary, many individuals are able to cope and fight off depression for years, until a precipitating stress comes along and wipes them out emotionally. Whenever depression is the result, the precipitating stresses (whatever they may be) have worked through repressed anger. Somehow, pent-up anger is always involved in any genuine clinical depression. Most precipitating stresses are brought on by our own very subtle, unconscious, self-destructive attitudes, emotions, and behavior patterns. However, life has plenty of stresses of its own for each of us to deal with, such as losing a loved one or facing up to our own death. None of the ten precipitating stresses discussed in this chapter will result in depression if we handle them responsibly. Irresponsible attitudes and actions will allow any of the ten to result in depression. Again we repeat, happiness is a choice.

11

What Are the Personality Dynamics that Lead to Depression?

This chapter is intended as a summary of some of the psychological and biological dynamics of depression not yet covered in this book. We trust that this summary will prove to be valuable not only to Christian counselors but to the lay person as well. We have already seen that some adults are more prone to depression than others because of unhealthy family patterns, especially in the first six years of life. One of the main factors is being taught in early childhood to repress anger rather than learning to express anger tactfully and constructively. A less important factor is heredity. The dynamics of obsessive-compulsive (perfectionistic) and hysterical (emotional) individuals have been outlined in the preceding chapters. All of these factors predispose a person to depression. Then, a precipitating stress comes along. A person who has applied the principles of this book to his life could handle any of these precipitating stresses without getting clinically depressed, even though he would have a temporary grief reaction. But a person who is predisposed by early environmental (and possibly hereditary) factors and who has learned to repress his anger will develop a full-blown depression. He will develop some of the physiological symptoms outlined in Chapter 2.

A Learned Pattern

Depression can become a learned pattern. In many families the parents are depressed; the children learn to identify with the parents and also develop the depressive type of life-style. Depression is learned as a way of life. It is learned as a way to handle stress. Depressed families can pass the depressive life-style from one generation to the next and to the next. Children do identify with parents and do become like them in their personalities and in the way they handle stressful situations. There is a segment of the brain known as the limbic area which is responsible for one's mood. It controls whether one feels elated or depressed or rather even in his temperament. Brain amines are neurotransmitters that float in the synapses between nerve cells. Depletion of these neurotransmitters (norepinephrine and serotonin) is felt to be a major factor in depression. Pent-up anger causes depletion of these amines. As a result the nervous system does not function properly and the individual may develop, among other things, insomnia, fatigue, appetite changes, or heart palpitations. Individuals who spend their entire childhood identifying with negativistic, chronically depressed parents are going to learn similar attitudes. Accordingly, they will have more than the average amount of pent-up anger, and their brain amines will be depleted much of the time. Some scientists speculate that the nervous system adjusts to this depressive life-style by staying somewhat depleted, by getting into a "biological rut," as it were. If this speculation proves true, medication to restore these brain amines would be very important to cure depression in these individuals. But an ounce of prevention is worth a pound of cure, so let's be sure not to rear our own children in a depressive life-style.

Manipulation

In certain cases depression becomes a way in which to deal with other people. In fact, depression can be a very powerful means of manipulating others and getting one's way. Individuals may use depression to manipulate their mate. Children may use depression as a way to manipulate their parents. Children should be encouraged to share their feelings, but not allowed to manipulate others by acting sad.

A Conscience Pleaser

In depression, the self is turned against the self. Thus, when one feels depressed and miserable he feels as though he is getting what he deserves. This appeases and pleases his conscience. It is self-inflicted emotional pain which appeases the punitive conscience. Therapy will be discussed later, but these individuals need to be taught that if any punishment is to be carried out, they should let God do it and stop punishing themselves. God may choose to discipline them, but if He does, that is His business and not theirs.

A Thought Disorder

As one becomes depressed, his thinking becomes progressively more and more painful. In other words, he feels more and more hopeless, helpless, worthless, and guilty. He becomes very self-critical and self-debasing. Thus, in general the theory is that as one develops depression, he develops painful thinking. It's a cycle. Inappropriate thinking results in more inappropriate thinking, and so on. Can an individual begin to change the way he feels about himself by changing what he is saying to himself? Patients often feel they have significantly improved when they change the way they talk to themselves. They feel it really helps to stop riding themselves so hard, and being so critical of themselves. When a depressed individual receives praise from twenty people and receives criticism from one, he will often focus on the criticism from the one individual and forget the praises from the twenty. He should be encouraged to reverse this trend, to begin to think on the positive feedback of others, and not on the less significant and less frequent negative feedback he has received.

Inappropriate Reward Systems

Children learn to respond to what they are rewarded for or disciplined for in childhood. For example, if when a child gets depressed he is rewarded by being permitted to stay home from school and given extra attention, he will tend to develop depression as a life-style. He is being inappropriately rewarded for his depression, and this reinforces it.

Hypothyroidism

Hypothyroidism can cause depression.[1] Many general practitioners have known for years that in certain (rare) cases of depression, thyroid medication seems to help.[2] This includes not only depressions caused by hypothyroidism but also some other cases of depression. Thyrotropin-releasing hormone (TRH_6) seems to help in some cases. Scientists suspect that depression can affect the thyroid gland sometimes and contribute to the development of hypothyroidism. It is well known that mind and body are intimately related, but it is not always known what comes first. It is our belief that with proper emotional and spiritual maturity most physical illnesses can be nearly eliminated from our lives.

Hypoglycemia

Hypoglycemia has been overstressed in our present-day culture. Many books have been written about hypoglycemia. Fatigue, depression, and just about every other malady have been attributed to hypoglycemia. This overemphasis has made the more conservative medical population skeptical. Hypoglycemia does exist, can cause increased anxiety, and can add to existing emotional problems. However, it should not be used to explain away most cases of anxiety or depression. For every actual incidence of hypoglycemia in the general population there are probably a hundred hysterical individuals and depressed individuals who, wishing to explain away their depression in something other than psychological or spiritual terms, attribute their problems to "hypoglycemia."

Biogenic Amine Imbalance

We have already mentioned that brain amines are neurotransmitters that float in the synapsis between two nerve cells. A decrease in these neurotransmitters is felt to be a major factor in depression.[3] There are several grounds to support this hypothesis:

1. A number of years ago a drug known as reserpine was used as a treatment for hypertension (high blood pressure). It was observed that a number of people on reserpine became depressed. It is now known that reserpine drugs deplete the brain amines. Not only will drugs containing reserpine cause symptoms of depression in man, but laboratory experiments have shown they also cause symptoms of depression when they are given to animals.
2. Drugs used in the treatment of depression are known to increase the level of brain amines. Apparently when these brain amines reach a normal level, the depression or many aspects of the depression disappear. Experiments have shown that these drugs can cause animals to become overly alert and restless. In other words, there is a lifting of their mood.
3. The level of catacholamine metabolites (the breakdown products of the biogenic amines) is found to be low in the urine of people who are significantly depressed.
4. To be added to the evidence that depression may be biological in nature is the fact that somatic symptoms do occur when depression exists. For example, such symptoms as disturbance of sleep, disturbance of appetite, disturbance of sex drive and so forth are present. It has also been found that depression is often associated with certain medical illnesses, for example, metabolic disorders. This would further substantiate the hypothesis that there are biological factors in depression.

5. The brain amine that has received most attention in America is norepinephrine. From the studies on norepinephrine has come the "catacholamine hypothesis of depression." This theory states that depression is a result of a depletion of this brain amine. This is probably somewhat of an oversimplification of what is actually going on. Further research has suggested that other brain amines may also be involved in certain cases of depression. For example, European studies have emphasized more the disturbance of the serotonin level. It is probable that in some cases of depression the norepinephrine is depleted and thus there is a response to drugs such as Tofranil which increase the level of norepinephrine. In other cases of depression the serotonin is depleted and there is a response drug such as Sinequan, which increases the level of serotonin. Tofranil probably increases the level of both norepinephrine and serotonin, so it is used more often than most other antidepressants.

Endocrine Imbalance

It has been known for some time that there is an association between depression and endocrine disorders.[4] Because of recent intense research into this area, the relationship is becoming more clear. The pituitary gland is known as the master gland and releases such hormones as ACTH (adrenocorticotropic hormone), growth hormone, luteinizing hormone, prolactin, and thyroid stimulating hormone. In reality, "master gland" is probably a misnomer because now we know that the pituitary gland is actually controlled by the nearby hypothalamus. Both glands are in the brain and are only about the size of a small marble. The hypothalamus secretes releasing factors, which cause the pituitary to release the above-mentioned hormones. It is further known that these releasing factors from the hypothalamus are controlled by biogenic amines such as norepinephrine. Of course, this is the chemical that is known to be depleted in cases of depression. Thus, if there is a disturbance in the biogenic amines in the brain, depression results, and there also may be an endocrine abnormality. This has indeed been proven to be the case. It has been found that in cases of depression there is an elevation of cortisol (stress hormone) levels in the blood. When cortisol levels are increased, lymphocytes (certain white blood cells) are suppressed. Lymphocytes produce antibodies. With *fewer antibodies*, the individual becomes more susceptible to nearly all physical illnesses. In other words, pent-up anger results in decreased norepinephrine, which results in increased ACTH releasing factor from the hypothalamus, which results in increased ACTH from the pituitary gland, which results in increased cortisol release from the adrenal gland (near the kidneys), which results in decreased lymphocytes, which results in decreased antibodies, which results in susceptibility to nearly all infectious diseases. *Pent-up anger is probably the leading cause of death*.

It has also been found that there is a possible lowering of the level of the luteinizing hormone and growth hormone. It is well known that decreased libido (sex drive) is a common occurrence in depression. This may be because of the effect of the endocrine system on the sex hormones. It is also interesting that when thyrotrophic (thyroid) releasing factors are administered to some individuals there is a temporary alleviating of depressive symptoms. All of these data support the hypothesis that there is an inner relationship between depression, low levels of brain amines such as norepinephrine, and an endocrine disturbance.

Electrolyte Disturbances

An electrolyte disturbance often occurs in depressive disorders.[5] For example, a disturbance in the distribution of sodium and potassium has been found in both depressed and manic patients. Whether this disturbance is primary or secondary is unclear. That is, whether it is causing the depression or a result of the depression is unclear (probably the latter). Electrolytes seem to play an important role in the synthesis, storage, release, and inactivation of neurotransmitters such as norepinephrine, which is a factor in depression. Changes in electrolyte distribution could arise in several ways. For example, sodium distribution is affected by such hormones as cortisol and aldosterone. Cortisol, in turn, is affected by the level of biogenic amines such as norepinephrine. Which affects the other first is still problematical and should provide for interesting research. One final evidence that electrolytes are involved in affective disorders is the fact that lithium carbonate salts have a dramatic effect in the treatment of manic-depressive disorders. The exact effect of this lithium salt on the electrolyte metabolism is not clear. It may have an influence upon the "sodium pump" activity in the kidneys.

Viral Infections

Depression often accompanies viral illness. Even when one has a relatively minor upper respiratory infection that is caused by a virus, he may note that he is also somewhat depressed. This is on a physical, biochemical level. Temporary viral illnesses can cause a temporary depressionlike syndrome. As stated previously, depression can also make one more susceptible to all infectious illnesses, including viral illnesses. Many cancers are now known to have a viral etiology.

Fatigue

One of the most common causes of depression is the rather common problem of fatigue. As one becomes overextended physically and emotionally, depression may be the result. In I Kings 19, it is recorded that Elijah became depressed when he overextended himself physically and emotionally. He became depressed to the point that he wanted to die. Many students have experienced the depression that is associated with staying up all night to study or trying to get by on five or six hours of sleep for many nights in a row. Ignoring our need for sleep is a sin, because our body is the temple of God. The average person needs eight hours of sleep per night. We also need time to dream to maintain our sanity. *All adults dream* about twenty minutes out of every ninety that they sleep, but they don't remember their dreams unless they wake up during one. Three nights without dreaming (even with plenty of sleep) will cause most people to get depressed and also somewhat paranoid. And which brain chemicals initiate and maintain dreaming? Recent research studies have proven that norepinephrine and serotonin (especially from the median raphe of the medulla oblongata at the base of the brain) initiate and maintain dreaming. In our dreams, all of our current unconscious conflicts are symbolized. Every dream has symbolic meaning. Dreams are usually unconscious wish-fulfillments in symbolic form. Thus, if an individual chooses happiness, he must also choose healthy sleep habits. Sleeping and dreaming are *necessary* to maintain life and sanity.

Depression in Adolescents

When adults become depressed they look depressed and act depressed. However, when adolescents become depressed, their depression is presented in a somewhat atypical manner. Instead of looking and acting depressed, they may act out their depression. Very moral, conscientious teen-agers may begin to steal, to lie, to take illegal drugs, or to misbehave sexually as a result of being depressed emotionally. Take the case of a girl brought in by her mother for treatment because she was misbehaving sexually and using drugs. The girl had been a very moral young lady until recent months. After learning that her daughter was depressed, the mother was given some limits to set for the girl. The daughter was given therapy and antidepressant medication. Within a matter of a few weeks she was again the conscientious young lady she had been previously. Hundreds of adolescents have been treated in a similar manner. This treatment *would not work*, however, in adolescents who have been spoiled, and have been misbehaving all their lives.

Children often become depressed after their parents divorce. They too act out their depression. When the anger they feel toward their parents because of the divorce is talked out, and the parents are forgiven (whether they deserve forgiveness or not), the children improve. Further, adolescents who misbehave and use drugs after their father's death begin to improve as soon as they are able to talk about his death and their feelings.

Postpartum Depression

It is not uncommon for a woman to become severely depressed after the birth of her baby.[6] This postpartum depression occurs most often in mothers who repress their mixed feelings about having the baby. Having mixed feelings is normal. Having a baby and mothering it for life is an enormous responsibility. If fears about having the baby are unacceptable to a mother and she represses these feelings, she will become depressed. It would be so much easier simply to admit these fears and discuss them with her husband or another female. The mother may express her ambivalent feelings symbolically by developing a fear of harming the baby. This is quite common. As a mother is able to discuss these feelings, her depression will usually lift, but antidepressant medications may sometimes be necessary as well.

Depression in Middle Life

Depression in middle life is very common.[7] It is particularly common in obsessive-compulsive individuals who feel they will never obtain the goals that they have set for themselves. Realizing this, they become very angry at themselves and clinically depressed.

Many losses can occur during middle life. For example, research has shown that a woman's greatest fear in her middle life is that she will lose her looks. Research has also shown that her second greatest fear is that she will lose her mate or that she will be alone. In addition to these losses, a woman may lose her children as they leave home. She may also lose the attention her husband had given her in earlier years. When she reacts to these losses, she becomes depressed.

Men also become depressed in middle life and may express this through improper sexual conduct. As though to prove to themselves that they are not losing their youth, they often are attracted to a younger female. This is the result of severe insecurity—they deceive themselves into believing that they are not losing their youth. Thus, the depression of middle life may be expressed by sexual misbehavior. It may also be expressed in an increased use of alcohol, in weight gain, or in the usual symptoms of depression listed previously.

Depression and the Elderly

In the elderly, we often see an accentuation of basic personality traits. Thus, the individual who has been somewhat depressed all of his life can expect to be *more* depressed as he gets older. In contrast, if he is a person who has a positive outlook on life and whose self-worth is based on godly wisdom, he will become happier and wiser the older he gets because his self-worth is still growing. His basic needs (self-worth, intimacy with others, and intimacy with God) continue to be met. In fact, they are fulfilled more completely than before. In old age, our inhibitions are decreased because of loss of certain brain cells, so increased guilt can be a problem. Elderly people also become depressed because they become lonely. They often suffer the loss of their mate and depression results. In this case it is a good idea to have friends of the same sex for fellowship.

To Get Even

Many people use their depression as a mechanism by which to vent their anger on and get even with others. By venting their anger in this manner, they may relieve their own anger to a degree, but they make others miserable. Living with a chronically depressed person would be quite punishing, and this is frequently the depressed mate's unconscious intent. We ask these depressed patients to think of better ways to get even with their mates (the suggestion is facetious, of course). Then we encourage them to work through their anger and forgive their mates so they can give up their depression.

Attention-Seeking Behavior

Individuals often use their depression as a means to gain attention from others. This is similar to using depression to manipulate others (which we have already discussed). Indeed, depression will gain a person much attention initially. However, it often backfires on the depressed individual and causes him more trouble later when his family and friends become frustrated in trying to deal with him. Attention-seeking depressions frequently end up in the loss of mate *and* friends. Then a really severe depression follows.

Masked Depression

A term that became popular in the 1950s is "masked depression."[8] It is characterized by somatic or physical complaints that seem to have no real basis in organic pathology. This condition responds readily to antidepressive medication. These somatic complaints may be headaches or various body aches and pains. As stated earlier, people transfer their emotional conflicts into physical complaints in order to deceive themselves into thinking they don't have any emotional conflicts. This is a face-saving defense mechanism.

Life Changes

Recently a young man could not understand why he was depressed. He had had a number of life changes in the past year. In fact, when he added up the total number of "life change units" he had experienced, he came up with more than 400. Researchers have found that an accumulation of 200 or more life change units in a single year is followed by a significant increase in psychiatric disorders. See the chart "The Stress of Adjusting to Change," which was developed by Homes and Rahe.[9]

One change that causes stress and is actually a kind of loss is a change of residence. Children that are subjected to repeated moves often become depressed.

As can be seen in the table, the change that causes the most stress is the death of a spouse, parent, or other close relative. In fact, the mortality rate increases markedly during the first year of bereavement.[10]

Children suffer the most when faced with the loss of a parent. They may show this by overt depression, by misconduct, or by clinging behavior. The more insecure a child feels, the more he may cling to those who remain. He may also be more subject to depression later in life.[11]

Human beings resist change. In fact, depressive individuals will often continue familiar patterns which cause them great discomfort. (At the same time these individuals may continually complain about these conditions.) For example, a masochistic and depressive woman may divorce a sadistic man only to turn around and marry another sadistic man. Her history may reveal that her parents were also sadistic. As she grew up, others imposed upon her and treated her unfairly. She did not like this, but it became a familiar pattern—one which she tries to continue in her present-day life.

THE STRESS OF ADJUSTING TO CHANGE[1]

Events	Scale of Impact
Death of a spouse	100
Divorce	73
Marital separation	65
Jail term	63
Death of close family member	63
Personal injury or illness	53
Marriage	50
Fired at work	47
Marital reconciliation	45
Retirement	45
Change in health of family member	44
Pregnancy	40
Sex difficulties	39
Gain of new family member	39
Business readjustment	39
Change in financial state	38
Death of close friend	37
Change to different line of work	36
Change in number of arguments with spouse	35
Mortgage over $10,000	31
Foreclosure of mortgage or loan	30
Change in responsibilities at work	29
Son or daughter leaving home	29
Trouble with in-laws	29
Outstanding personal achievement	28
Wife begins or stops work	26
Begin or end school	26
Change in living conditions	25
Revision of personal habits	24
Trouble with boss	23
Change in work hours or conditions	20
Change in residence	20
Change in schools	20
Change in recreation	19
Change in church activities	19
Change in social activities	18
Mortgage or loan less than $10,000	17
Change in sleeping habits	16
Change in number of family get-togethers	15
Change in eating habits	15
Vacation	13
Christmas	12
Minor violations of the law	11

[1] © 1967 by Pergamon Press, Inc.

Depression Viewed from Various Angles

There are ten major classifications of depression in the psychiatric literature. These ten classifications are described in Appendix 1 for those who are interested. However, let us now take a brief look at some of the other ways in which depression can be classified, such as spiritual versus psychological depression and endogenous versus exogenous depression.[12]

Unipolar Depression Versus Bipolar Depression. One way of classifying depression is as unipolar or bipolar. Unipolar depressions are characterized by mood shifts solely from an average, normal mood (a base-line mood) to a mood of depression. A bipolar depression is characterized by an alteration from an elated or manic state to a state of depression. Unipolar depressions are far more common than bipolar depressions. They seem to carry a less clear-cut genetic factor than do the bipolar depressions. The manic-depressive psychosis described above is bipolar. In the bipolar depression there is a history not only of depression but also of manic-type episodes during which the person is elated, may have very rapid speech and increased motor movement, may be extremely optimistic, and may show poor business or financial judgments. He may have delusions of grandeur, increase his sexual activity, be very talkative, and have periods of sleeplessness which last day and night. Manic and depressive episodes may be separated by a month or even by a period of many years.

Endogenous Depression Versus Exogenous Depression. Another classification for depression is endogenous versus exogenous. Endogenous depression refers to depression that comes from within. It is supposedly caused by a neurochemical imbalance rather than by a psychological conflict or environmental stress. This neurochemical imbalance may be genetic in origin. In contrast to this, exogenous depression (also known as reactive or situational depression) is caused by stressful situations in life. A loss of some kind is often found to be the cause. For example, there may be the loss of a loved one or there may be trouble at one's job. In short, the endogenous depression comes from a neurochemical imbalance within and the exogenous depression comes from situational conflicts from without.

Spiritual Depression Versus Psychological Depression Versus Physical Depression. Another way to classify depression is spiritual, psychological, or physical. Often the boundary is vague and the line between them is hard to distinguish. In fact, all three parts of man (spiritual, psychological, and physical) are often involved. When one is involved, usually the other two are also. For example, suppose that depression starts as a spiritual depression. An example would be a middle-aged male who commits adultery. He then becomes depressed because of true guilt. Psychological factors may enter in due to his particular personality. Perhaps he does not handle his guilt in an appropriate, healthy way because of past experiences. Instead of turning to the Lord, confessing his guilt, and getting his life straightened out, he may worry over the problem and become very depressed. In fact, he may worry to the point that he develops a chemical imbalance, and thus he develops physical depression also.

Factors that could precipitate a primarily spiritual type of depression include true guilt, anger turned inward, a wrong perspective, and an attack by Satan. Psychological depression could occur in someone who in early life learned patterns ill-equipping him to adapt to difficulties, or who was rewarded inappropriately as a child. Psychological depression could also occur when there is a thought disorder, when there has been a loss, and when false guilt is present. Among the factors that could trigger a physical depression are hypothyroidism, hypoglycemia, biogenic amine imbalance, electrolyte imbalance, endocrine imbalance, fatigue, and viral illnesses.

Organically Based Depressions. As stated previously, a depression can be caused by organic illness. For example, many viral illnesses can give a temporary depression, as will serious disorders such as malignancy. Depression can also be a result of medication. This is the case when individuals are treated with a drug known as reserpine for hypertension. The reserpine lowers the norepinephrine level in the brain and depression results. Depression can even be seen as a result of a stroke. Interestingly enough, strokes in the right cerebral hemisphere more often result in a degree of euphoria, whereas those on the left more often result in depression.

Endogenous Depression Versus Neurotic Depression Versus Reactive Depression. One of the latest ways of categorizing depression is endogenous, neurotic, or reactive. In considering this classification, perhaps it would be helpful to review the three basic factors present in the causation of psychological problems: heredity, early environment, and psychological problems (see the chart "Causes of Psychological Problems"). Each of these factors is so important that a book could be written about each one.

> Mental illness . . . often is not caused by one factor alone. A spiritual problem may be the cause of the emotional problem, but other factors often come into play or are responsible.
>
> For example, the genetic background is important when examining a mental problem. There is one mental problem in particular, manic-depressive psychosis, where an unusually high proportion of the relatives . . . also have the problem. Scientific studies have also documented that children of schizophrenic parents develop schizophrenia significantly more often than other children, even when they are raised away from the parents. Furthermore, one does not have to look far to see that personality traits run in families. Just as dogs pass on personality traits (German shepherd—aggressive, St. Bernard—friendly), so do humans.
>
> Secondly, the environmental background is of much importance in forming a personality. Children are taught to be humble, aggressive, polite, or rude. . . . Parents may wonder why their sixteen-year-old Johnny is rude, rebellious, and disobedient. Yet, the parents have never disciplined him. Physical health could also be included in this category. Children or adults who are physically ill usually have less capacity to withstand emotional stress.
>
> Usually, a third factor is necessary for a psychological problem to develop. This third factor is a precipitating stress. Although one may have hereditary factors present and may have had a difficult early environment, a psychological disorder may never develop unless he is in an acutely stressful situation.
>
> Truly, the genetic and environmental backgrounds are factors of major importance. To deny this is naive. However, it is equally naive to use these as excuses for present conduct. Many problems are brought about through irresponsible behavior. What the Apostle Paul said many years ago is still true:

Causes of Psychological Problems

Hereditary endowment

↓

Early environment →

- Birth to six years (social, religious, physical factors)
- Defense mechanisms to handle stress are developing. Personality traits are developing.
- If detrimental defense mechanisms develop, then a personality disorder develops here.

↓

Acutely stressful situation in the adult years →

- Neurosis
- Psychosis
- Psycho-physiologic disorder

↓

Healthy individual able to cope. He uses the Lord and other Christians as the major resources to help him.

> ". . . whatsoever a man soweth, that shall he also reap" (Galatians 6:7). Many times emotional problems are brought about through irresponsible behavior, sins, or just not knowing, or failing to rely on the resources that a Christian has at his disposal.[13]

If the emphasis is placed on the hereditary factor in depression, it is called an endogenous depression. This means it comes from within, is biochemical in nature, and, of course, is genetically induced.

If the emphasis is placed on the early environmental factors, it is called a neurotic depression. This means it arises from subconscious, unresolved conflicts of childhood.

If the emphasis is placed on the precipitating stress, it is called a reactive depression. This means it is caused by an overwhelming situational problem.

Personality Traits of the Depressed

Various personality traits are commonly seen in depressed individuals:

1. Worry.
2. Pessimism.
3. Low level of energy.
4. Sense of futility; feelings of uselessness.
5. Depressed mood.
6. Unhappiness.
7. Sadness.
8. Feelings of worthlessness.
9. Feelings of hopelessness.
10. Feelings of helplessness.
11. Thinking permeated by guilt.
12. Dwelling on the past.
13. Despondency.
14. Gloom.

15. Agitation.
16. Irritability.
17. Perplexity.
18. Feelings of inadequacy.
19. Lack of confidence.
20. Conviction that all endeavors are meaningless and without value.
21. Inability to concentrate.
22. Psychomotor retardation.
23. Decrease in body movement.
24. Decrease in thought processes.
25. Sad affect.
26. Sullen bitterness.
27. Anger.
28. Anxiety.
29. Hypochondria.
30. Sense of dread.
31. Sense of fear of dying.
32. Melancholia.
33. Loss of interest.
34. Attention completely turned inward.
35. Paralysis of the will.
36. Belief that *morning* is the worst part of the day.
37. Reluctance to get up in the morning.
38. Decrease in appetite or increase in appetite (usually decrease).
39. Loss of weight or increase in weight (usually loss).
40. Constipation.
41. Marked fatigue.

42. Coldness of extremities.
43. Insomnia (inability to sleep).
44. Difficulty falling asleep.
45. Increase in sleep (occasionally).
46. Early morning awakening.
47. Decrease in sex drive.
48. Dysmenorrhea (menstrual irregularities).
49. Amenorrhea (the menstrual cycle ceases for duration of depression).
50. Hot flashes.
51. Possibility of suicide.
52. Painful thinking (emotionally painful).
53. Loss of motivation, apathy.
54. False guilt.
55. Dejected or discouraged appearance.
56. Forehead furrowed.
57. Corners of mouth turned down.
58. Frequent desire to cry.
59. Unkempt or slovenly appearance.
60. Discontinuance of shaving (men).
61. Discontinuance of wearing make-up (women).
62. Strong superego.
63. Withdrawal.
64. Loss of sense of humor—difficulty laughing.
65. Living in the past—future looks dim.
66. Belief that life is not worth living.
67. Self-possession.
68. Introspection.
69. Introversion.

70. Loss of self-confidence.
71. Feelings of inferiority.
72. Physical symptoms: tension headaches, rapid heartbeat, infections, gastrointestinal disturbances.
73. Little enthusiasm.
74. Emptiness.
75. Longing.
76. Feelings of unreality.
77. Depersonalization (the feeling that one is unreal or is leaving his body).
78. Feelings of being unloved and mistreated.
79. Preoccupation with self.
80. Remorse.
81. Difficulty remembering joys of the past.
82. Little initiative or spontaneity.
83. Halting and uncertain speech.
84. Neckache.
85. Backache.
86. Dryness of mouth.
87. Limp handshake.
88. Low self-concept.
89. Craving for love from others.
90. Expectations of rejection.
91. Exaggerated expectations of others, but fear of rejection. This fear results in a vicious cycle: anger → withdrawal from possible close relationships → unsatisfied dependency needs → increased anger.
92. Feelings of isolation.
93. Clinging behavior.
94. Defenses of denial, displacement, introjection, projection, and somatization.

95. Desire to conceal aggression.
96. Feelings of being a "super person." These feelings occur prior to the fall into depression as a manic defense against becoming aware of one's low self-worth.
97. Possibility of paranoia. To increase one's self-esteem, he becomes grandiose and projects his hostility onto others. He becomes convinced they are angry at him, even though they aren't. He projects his anger onto them much as a slide projector projects a slide onto a screen.
98. Masochism—seeking painful experiences and the security of familiar masochistic patterns.
99. No enjoyment in recreation.
100. The object of the anger of other family members.
101. Member of a legalistic or an overly emotional church (the two extremes of spiritual immaturity discussed by Francis Schaeffer in his book, *The New Superspirituality*).

PART THREE

How Can One Overcome Depression?

12

Are There Some Basic Guidelines for a Happy Life?

To be remembered at this point are the three basic needs of all human beings: (1) self-worth; (2) intimacy with others; (3) intimacy with God. All three of these are included in the great commandment, summarized by Jesus Christ in Mark 12:29-31. The Bible indicates that all the other laws of Scripture hang on this great commandment—in other words, if we obey the great commandment, we automatically obey all the other commandments. What is that great commandment? Christ said, "You shall love the Lord your God with all your heart, and with all your soul, and with all your mind, and with all your strength. This is the first commandment. The second is this, you shall love your neighbor as yourself. There is no other commandment greater than these." Love God; love your neighbor; love yourself (genuine self-worth is the opposite of false pride, which is a terrible sin committed primarily by individuals who are trying to compensate for their lack of self-worth).

The seven basic guidelines in this chapter are all based on the great commandment. If any human chooses to live by these seven basic guidelines, we are convinced that he will go through life without ever suffering any of the pains of depression. Of course, he may still have some ups and downs, and still experience normal grief reactions just as all humans do, but he will *never* suffer from any symptoms of clinical depression.

One more essential bit of information must be added before discussing the "Seven Basic Guidelines." Without a vital personal relationship with Jesus Christ, no human will have the power within himself to consistently choose these seven basic guidelines. As psychiatrists we cringe whenever patients use the word *can't*. They say, for example, "I just *can't* get along with my husband." "My husband and I just *can't* communicate." "I *can't* seem to discipline my children the way I should." "I *can't* give up the affair I am having." "I *can't* find a job." "I *can't* stop overeating." "I *can't* love my wife—I've tried."

Any good psychiatrist knows that "I can't" and "I've tried" are merely lame excuses. We insist that our patients be honest with themselves and use language that expresses the reality of the situation. So we have our patients change their *can'ts* to *won'ts*. Let's substitute the word *won't* in each of the statements made above. "I just *won't* get along with my husband." "My husband and I just *will not* communicate." I *will not* discipline my children the way I should." "I *won't* give up the affair I'm having." "I *will not* find a job." "I *won't* stop overeating." "I *won't* love my wife—I'll make a halfhearted effort at loving her but I *won't* quite succeed."

If an individual changes all his *can'ts* to *won'ts*, he stops avoiding the truth, quits deceiving himself, and starts living in reality—*if* he is a Christian. The Bible tells Christians in Philippians 4:13, "I can do all things through Christ which strengtheneth me." In I Corinthians 10:13, Christians are told that they are *never tempted* to sin without simultaneously being provided with a way (and the power) to escape that sinful temptation. The Christian who continually fails is without excuse—he is defeating himself. He is his own worst enemy. The Christian who is depressed is depressed because he is *choosing* (either out of ignorance of the Word or else on purpose) to be depressed, choosing not to live by God's principles. Living by God's principles results in the fruits of the Spirit, which include love (rather than pent-up anger or bitterness), joy (rather than depression), and peace (rather than anxiety). Whoever does not have the fruits of the Spirit is not living by the Spirit.

Whenever a non-Christian patient uses the word *can't*, we let him get away with it, because we believe him. A non-Christian, without the power of God in his life, really *cannot* choose righteous paths consistently. We have treated over two thousand patients for depression, both Christians and non-Christians, and *all* of them get over their depression. Some take a full year to get over it instead of the usual two or three months, but all of them do get over their symptoms of clinical depression. But those who choose not to accept Christ as Savior do not have the power to stay out of depression. A year or so later they get back into the same rut. Christians who get over their depression and continue to follow our "Seven Basic Guidelines" *never* get depressed again.

Thus, the primary step to overcoming depression is to utilize the excellent resource that we have or can have in Christ. Christians are not without problems. In fact they have problems just like everyone else. However, they do have available an excellent resource to draw upon to solve their problems. To utilize Christ as a resource to help solve depression, an individual must first accept Christ as his Savior. To accept Christ, or believe in Christ, means basically two things. First, it means the individual knows certain facts; and, secondly, it means the individual has a personal relationship with Jesus Christ.

First, the individual must know certain facts. For example, he must know that Christ was more than just a good man. He is also the Son of God. He died on a cross for the sins of the world. In other words, He made payment in full to God for the sins of whoever would turn to Him. He not only died on the cross for our individual sins, but He also arose from the grave and was victorious over death. These are the basic facts about Christ which must be known by the individual. However, merely knowing these facts is not enough. The individual must also have a personal relationship with Christ. He must personally believe in Christ. The way in which one comes to personally believe in Christ may take different forms in different individuals. For example, one individual may ask Christ to be his Savior. Another individual may suddenly realize that Christ died for him and his sins. Whatever the case, the important thing is that there be a personal relationship with Christ.

Belief in Christ starts with a choice of the will. The degree of the emotional conviction involved in the choice will differ from individual to individual. We have counseled quite a few individuals who were concerned whether they had believed enough. They seemed to be confusing belief with full emotional persuasion. We shared with them that their belief starts with the will. Emotions are sometimes evasive and hard to change because they may be set in psychological problems and roots of many years past. For example, a woman who could never trust or depend on her parents may have trouble feeling that she can always trust and depend on God. Belief for her should begin with the will; later, as she spends time growing in Christ and in His Word, her emotions will also change and she will become fully convinced.

To repeat, belief must start with the will. Failure to accept this premise leads to the unresolvable problem of the degree of belief—what degree of belief or emotional persuasion does it take to save an individual? Where would the line be drawn, that is, the line determining whether belief is strong enough or still too weak? In Mark 9 is recorded the story of an epileptic boy. The father of the boy brought him to see Jesus. Jesus shared with the man that all things were possible if he believed. The man told Jesus that he did believe, but then he asked Him to help his unbelief. In other words, there were still some aspects to his emotions that were not fully convinced. However, with his will he was choosing to believe. It is interesting to note that in the Gospels alone the word *believe* (or its equivalent) is listed 115 times as the condition for salvation. In this connection consider the following verses from the New Testament:

> And he said to the woman, Thy faith hath saved thee; go in peace. (Luke 7:50)
>
> But as many as received him, to them gave he power to become the children of God, even to them that believe on his name. (John 1:12)
>
> For God so loved the world, that he gave his only begotten Son, that whosoever believeth in him should not perish, but have everlasting life. (John 3:16)
>
> And [the Philippian jailer] brought them [Paul and Silas] out, and said, Sirs, what must I do to be saved? And they said, Believe on the Lord Jesus Christ, and thou shalt be saved, and thy house. (Acts 16:30, 31)
>
> For the wages of sin is death; but the gift of God is eternal life through Jesus Christ our Lord. (Romans 6:23)
>
> For whosoever shall call upon the name of the Lord shall be saved. (Romans 10:13)
>
> For by grace are ye saved through faith, and that not of yourselves, it is the gift of God: Not of works, lest any man should boast. (Ephesians 2:8, 9)
>
> Who hath saved us, and called us with an holy calling, not according to our works, but according to his own purpose and grace, which was given us in Christ Jesus before the world began. (II Timothy 1:9)
>
> Wherefore, he is able also to save them to the uttermost that come unto God by him, seeing he ever liveth to make intercession for them. (Hebrews 7:25)

To believe is simply to realize what Christ has done for us and to accept His death on the cross in our place for the punishment of our sins. This is all that is required of any sinner in coming to Christ. Perhaps it would be helpful to describe what belief is not. Belief is not a public acknowledgement of Christ, although the two can occur at the same time. Belief is not prayer, although one can express belief in prayer. Belief is not repentance, although repentance does occur simultaneously with belief. Belief is not confession of sin, although as one realizes his sin and that Christ is the only atonement for that sin, he may want to talk to the Lord about his sin. In summary, belief is simply realizing that Christ died for our sins, and trusting Him to save us. Trusting Christ is a matter of the will—salvation, like happiness, is a choice. God does all the work, through Christ's atonement and the Holy Spirit's conviction—we humans merely choose to accept salvation or we choose to reject it. To be passive about salvation is the same as choosing to reject it. And according to John 3:16-18 and scores of other passages, eternal damnation awaits those who actively or passively reject Jesus Christ as Savior.

Once an individual accepts Christ, he does have available to him a tremendous resource that he did not have before, since Christ becomes his brother and God the Father becomes his personal father. Most earthly fathers desire to help their children, and in like manner, and much more so, God desires to help His children when they suffer in any way, especially in depression.

Let's turn our attention now to those seven basic guidelines for a happy, fulfilling and meaningful life, discussing what is meant by each one of them. Again, the reader should recall that all seven of these are based on the great commandment and all seven help us to meet our three basic human needs (self-worth, intimacy with others, and intimacy with God).

1. *Commit your life daily to the purpose of glorifying Jesus Christ.*

We commit our lives to glorifying Christ the first thing each morning. We wake up and thank God for another day to enjoy life. We pray that God will use us that day to bring glory to Him by benefiting our fellow man (including our wives and children). We pray for self-control (through His strength) to overcome the temptations of the day, and we ask Him to forgive us when we do make mistakes, realizing that all Christians (including ourselves) do make mistakes daily. As we go through the events of the day, we are reminded that we have committed that day to the pursuit of God and His glory. Realizing this helps us to love our patients more—to be more tolerant—to have genuine Christlike concern. We have even wept at times over the sufferings of some of our more seriously ill patients. Committing the day to God also helps us to love ourselves more and not to be so self-critical. It also helps us to love our wives, children, and friends more, as we think of ways we can benefit them for the glory of God.

2. *Spend some time each day meditating on God's Word and applying it to your life.*

Our brains are just like computers, *except* for the fact that we have a *will* and computers have no will of their own. Since we are born with a selfish, self-deceiving sinful nature, we tend to automatically do the wrong things much of the time—things that lead to depression and self-destruction. Not only do we do those things, but we also deny that we are doing them. Again recall the words of the prophet Jeremiah (17:9), who said, "The heart is deceitful above all things, and desperately wicked: who can know it?" If we choose happiness, we *must* choose also to reprogram our "computer" brains to God's way of thinking instead of our own crazy way of thinking. We can do this only by frequent meditation on God's Word.

A neurosurgeon by the name of Penfield conducted experiments using electrodes in certain areas of the brain.[1] By touching the electrodes to certain areas of the brain he found that individuals would recall past events. Not only were they able to recall the events, but they were also able to recall the feelings that occurred along with those events in years past. Sometimes individuals would just recall certain feelings without remembering the specific event. From this we can deduce that the brain acts as a computer: sometimes it records memories, sometimes feelings, and sometimes both memories and feelings. We can also deduce that what was recorded is available for replay today and may influence much of our present-day behavior. Thus, *bad programming from the past* can affect our present-day attitudes. It can affect the way we go around talking to ourselves during the day, and thus how we feel. It can cause us to utilize depression *as a means to gain attention*. It can cause us to use depression *as a way to manipulate others*. It can cause us to be *negative in our thought patterns* throughout the day. It can cause us *to worry constantly* from moment to moment. It can cause us *to have painful thinking* that reinforces a depressed mood. It can cause us *to be filled with self-doubt* and criticism. It can cause us *to doubt our personal relationship* with the Lord, and it can cause us to *question our relationship* with and acceptance by other people.

We have very little direct control today over what was programmed years ago, but we can begin to reprogram our computer.

According to John 3:6, when an individual becomes a Christian, he has a new spirit within him. In other words, the Holy Spirit comes to indwell him. Thus, he has a new potential resource to solve his problems. It is important to note that it is the spirit which becomes new, and not necessarily the mind, emotions, or will. The mind, emotions, and will are transformed only over a period of time as one spends time in prayer with God, in fellowship with other Christians, and in meditation on the Word of God.

In Romans 12:2, the apostle Paul states that we should not be conformed to this world but that we should be transformed by the renewing of our minds. This renewing of the mind is a gradual process that begins at the time of acceptance of Christ (at the time of the new birth) and of the indwelling by the Holy Spirit (which occurs at the very moment we come to trust Christ). This renewing of the mind is not a once-for-all phenomenon. It begins at the time of the new birth and continues throughout life. If the mind has had a substantial amount of bad programming during the early years, it may take many years to reprogram it in a more healthy direction. However, it can be reprogrammed.

First of all, the mind can be *reprogrammed by using the Word of God*. In Isaiah 55:11 God proclaims: "So shall my word be that goeth forth out of my mouth; it shall not return unto me void, but it shall accomplish that which I please, and it shall prosper in the thing whereto I sent it." God's Word will accomplish the purpose that He desires. His Word can reprogram our mind. David asserted that God's testimonies (that is to say, God's Word) were his counselors. When Moses was speaking to the children of Israel, he told them that the words he was speaking were not vain, but were the very life of the children of God (Deuteronomy 32:46, 47). God's Word, then, should be our very life. Joshua recorded the way to success: "This book of the law shall not depart out of thy mouth, but thou shalt meditate therein day and night, that thou mayest observe to do according to all that is written therein; for then thou shalt make thy way prosperous, and then thou shalt have good success" (Joshua 1:8). In Psalm 1, King David compared a mentally healthy man to a tree growing by a river: "But his delight is in the law of the Lord; and in his law doth he meditate day and night. And he shall be like a tree planted by the rivers of water, that bringeth forth its fruit in its season; its leaf also shall not wither; and whatsoever he doeth shall prosper." In other words, when troubles come, the man of God can remain stable and survive because of his having been programmed with his reliance on the Word of God. Christ stated that man shall not live by bread alone, but by every word that proceedeth out of the mouth of God (Matthew 4:4). Furthermore, if we abide in Christ, and His Word abides in us, we can ask whatsoever we will, and it shall be done unto us (John 15:7). In other words, the Word of God does have an amazing transforming power—it can reprogram our computer.

In Colossians 3:16 the apostle Paul encouraged the church to let the Word of God indwell them richly. In Jeremiah 15:16, the prophet noted that God's words were found, and that he "ate them," and that they were unto him the joy and rejoicing of his soul. The Word of God can give joy to help counteract depression. It can reprogram our computer. In I John 2:14 the apostle noted that he was writing to young men who were strong and in whom the Word of God was abiding. They were strong emotionally precisely because the Word of God was abiding in them. They had reprogrammed their computer according to the Word of God and, therefore, they were strong and stable emotionally.

Another way we can reprogram our computer (or at least stop reinforcing bad programming) is to *monitor what we are thinking*. Critical and negative thinking reinforces a depressed mood. An individual can help to lift his mood by changing the way he thinks. In Philippians 4:8 the apostle Paul encouraged his readers to think on things that were true, honest, just, pure, lovely, of good report, and things that were worthy of virtue and praise. This type of thinking tends to lift the mood whereas negative and critical thinking tends to reinforce an already depressed mood. There really is power in positive thinking!

We can learn much about the pursuit of God by meditating on His Word. A very good example is the story of King Hezekiah. II Kings 18 gives insight concerning how to have self-control and be in pursuit of God. King Hezekiah kept the Lord's commandments. He knew the Word of God, he loved it, and he kept it. Perhaps Christ Himself stated the principle best in Matthew 4:4: "It is written, Man shall not live by bread alone, but by every word that proceedeth out of the mouth of God." And in John 6:63 Christ stated: "It is the spirit that quickeneth; the flesh profiteth nothing: the words that I speak unto you, they are spirit, and they are life." Finally, in I John 2:14 is recorded: "I have written unto you, fathers, because ye have known him that is from the beginning. I have written unto you, young men, because ye are strong, and the word of God abideth in you, and ye have overcome the wicked one." As pointed out previously, the young men were strong because the Word of God abided in them. And then as the years passed they too would eventually be characterized as were their fathers—men who knew God, men who were in pursuit of God. Indeed, no one will ever be a man of God unless he is a man of the Book.

There is yet another element mentioned in II Kings 18 that relates to being in pursuit of God. It is more than just self-control; it is more than knowing the Bible. It is the element of "cleaving" to the Lord (II Kings 18:6). Many Christians have accomplished much for the Lord because of their self-control and because of their ardent study of the Book. However, there are only a few Christians who go on to the third and most important factor: the matter of "cleaving to the Lord." The Hebrew word for "cleave" here (II Kings 18:6) is the very word that is used in Genesis 2:24 ("a man shall leave his father and his mother, and shall cleave unto his wife"). It implies a friendship. It implies a longing to be with someone. It implies enjoyment in being with that someone, and it implies spending much time together. To cleave to God implies that we are intensely in pursuit of Him. It means that we desire to spend time with Him, to walk with Him and talk with Him, to know Him as we would any other friend, and to be close to Him.

Specifically, how can we be in pursuit of God? Well, let's look again at King Hezekiah. In II Chronicles 29:11 Hezekiah said to the Levites, "My sons, be not now negligent: for the Lord hath chosen you to stand before him, to serve him, and that ye should minister unto him, and burn incense." King Hezekiah was suggesting to the Levites that they spend time with the Lord and that they, in fact, should talk to the Lord about the Lord. The application to be drawn from this is that in our quiet times with the Lord, we ought to spend time talking to God about God. How much time have we spent in the last week talking to God just about God, about how we appreciate Him, *our friend*?

In II Chronicles 29:20 it is recorded: "Then Hezekiah the king rose early, and gathered the rulers of the city, and went up to the house of the Lord." The application here is that it takes time to be in pursuit of God. It takes time to develop a friendship; it takes time spent together for closeness to grow. One of the marks of our day is that men desire a short cut in knowing God. They go off on various tangents, such as "experiential hysterics," in efforts to find a short cut. But there is no short cut to knowing someone. Time is required, and King Hezekiah was willing to spend time with the Lord.

In verse 30 it is recorded: "Moreover Hezekiah the king and the princes commanded the Levites to sing praise unto the Lord with the words of David, and of Asaph the seer. And they sang praises with gladness, and they bowed their heads and worshipped." The application here is that time spent in singing songs to the Lord about Himself can aid us in knowing the Lord. There are relatively few hymns that are songs to the Lord. Most of them are songs about the Lord. It is good to sing songs to the Lord just about Him. This is real worship. The verse under consideration states that the Levites sang praises with gladness and they gathered in worship. It can be a most rewarding experience to search through hymnbooks for hymns which are sung directly to the Lord.

In II Chronicles 30:8 we read,"Now be ye not stiffnecked, as your fathers were, but yield yourselves unto the Lord, and enter into his sanctuary, which he hath sanctified for ever: and serve the Lord your God, that the fierceness of his wrath may turn away from you." The fourth principle to be drawn from Hezekiah is that we should exercise self-control to assure that nothing will keep us from the pursuit of our God. This self-control in turn will give us a sound mind (see II Timothy 1:7).

In II Chronicles 31:21 it is recorded, "And in every work that he began in the service of the house of God, and in the law, and in the commandments, to seek his God, he did it with all his heart, and prospered." The final lesson to be drawn from King Hezekiah is that he sought God with all his heart. To be in pursuit of God, we need to seek Him with all our heart, determine that we are going to build a relationship with Him, that we are going to know Him intimately, and that we are going to know Him better than any friend here on earth.

In thinking about this principle, a young person might imagine that God picks certain men to whom He reveals Himself intimately—men with whom He walks and to whom He is very close. But as the years pass, it becomes clear that God does not work that way. God is already in pursuit of us and He is looking for men who will be in pursuit of Him. "For the eyes of the Lord run to and fro throughout the whole earth, to shew himself strong in the behalf of them whose heart is perfect toward him" (II Chronicles 16:9). God is already in pursuit of us and He searches to the ends of the earth with His eyes to find men who are being diligent in pursuing Him. To those men, He reveals Himself. And with those men, He develops and cultivates an intimate relationship. That is the kind of relationship that King Hezekiah had with God. He was a man in pursuit of God. God was accordingly pleased. God desires the same of us today.

3. *Get rid of grudges daily.*

Ephesians 4:26 advises getting rid of grudges daily. This will prevent clinical depression from ever developing. This counsel is so vitally important that an entire chapter (chapter 13) is devoted to principles on how to deal with anger. (Study of these principles should be delayed until the material in the present chapter is understood thoroughly.)

4. *Spend a little time nearly every day getting more intimate with your mate and children. Parents, brothers, sisters, and other close relatives should also have a high priority. Do all you can to resolve family conflicts.*

Don't ever get vengeance on family members. Heal the

wounds the best you can and leave the rest up to God. Intimacy with your family is more vital to your self-worth and overall mental health than most people imagine. Unresolved family conflicts can continue for years and years. The word *family* in this case is to be understood in a far broader sense than one's immediate relatives. A good example in today's world is the continual "family feud" between the Arabs and Israelis. Their sibling rivalry has been waged off and on for several thousand years. If their family conflicts had been resolved several thousand years ago, when they should have been, the Arabs and Israelis would still be intimate friends today instead of bitter enemies.

Though the practice of psychiatry keeps us very busy, we both spend an average of two hours each weeknight and four hours each Saturday and Sunday playing with our own children. The old saying, "It's not the quantity but the quality of time spent with your children that's important," is nonsense! The quantity of time is just as important as the quality of time. We also take time every day to communicate with our wives on a deep and intimate level. We also take our wives out on dates at least once or twice each week. And we are frequently thinking of things to do that will cultivate intimate friendships with our parents, brothers, sisters, and other close relatives.

As much as we humans hate to admit it, much of our self-worth is based on our parents' love and acceptance of us. We must take the initiative ourselves in resolving old family conflicts. We must not keep at a distance until our relatives "repent" for hurting our feelings. The most mature thing we can do is to assume 100 percent of the responsibility for resolving family conflicts, then pray that we can discover creative ways in which to achieve reconciliation. If these efforts fail, we must try new measures.

5. *Spend some time each week having fellowship and fun with at least one or two committed Christian friends of the same sex. If you are married, have fun with other married couples. In this way husband and wife can together benefit from intimacy with others.*

In Proverbs 13:20 Solomon states, "He who walks with wise men will be wise, but the companion of fools will suffer harm."

Select your friends very carefully, because *you will become more and more like your friends whether you intend to or not*! Share your burdens with your friends (see Hebrews 10:24, 25). You should have a few non-Christian friends as well, but *if you are a committed Christian*, you will want your most intimate friends to be committed Christians also. Don't overestimate your own spiritual strength. It is much easier than most Christians think for a non-Christian friend to bring a Christian down spiritually. In Proverbs 27:17, wise King Solomon wrote that "as iron sharpens iron, so a man sharpens the countenance of his friend." He also wrote that a merry heart does good like a medicine (Proverbs 17:22). The lesson in this is to cultivate friendships with happy Christians who are enjoying the fruits of Christian maturity. Don't become too intimate with immature Christians who are continually wallowing in their own depressive attitudes toward life and their own self-pity.

No man is an island. No man can be a happy hermit. Loneliness is painful. We *must* have intimate friends. Again, we must assume *100 percent* of the responsibility for building friendships. Solomon said that if we want friends, we must go out and be friendly—we have to earn friends. All humans fear rejection—some more than others. Don't expect everyone to like you. Make friendly gestures toward three or four couples, and if only one of them responds, consider that a successful average. You don't need a great number of friends. You need two or three intimate friends. Then, if one dies, moves away, or rejects you later, it won't be a total disaster for you. You will still have a couple intimate friends on whom to lean. Solomon said, "A man of many friends comes to ruin, but there is a friend who sticks closer than a brother" (Proverbs 18:24). Intimacy is what is needed here, not quantity. And be sure never to hold a grudge against any friend. Grudges will accumulate easily; if you don't verbalize and resolve your anger, you will eventually take it out in unconscious ways. Solomon said, "He who covers a transgression seeks love, but he who repeats a matter separates intimate friends" (Proverbs 17:9).

6. *Be involved in a daily routine (including work, play, housework, projects) that brings personal satisfaction to you. Be convinced that this*

routine is God's will and purpose for your life–your way of glorifying Him.

God doesn't call everyone into full-time Christian work. Many young Christians are naive about this. And being in full-time Christian work does not make anyone more spiritual than a committed Christian who digs ditches for a living. In heaven, there will be reverses in status that will surprise many Christians because the first will be last and the last first. As Christian physicians who teach at a seminary and write books, we get much recognition. But both of us know many very committed Christians, real prayer warriors, who get very little public recognition. In heaven, we will be happy if we are allowed to sweep the front porches of some of our unrecognized but intensely spiritual friends. Christ said in John 10:10 that His purpose in coming to earth was not only to save man, but also to enable man to live an abundant (fulfilling) life. Pray for God's guidance, but depend on His Word to give you that guidance. Don't make major decisions on the basis of your whimsical emotions and then blame those decisions on the Holy Spirit. It is disheartening to hear immature Christians say, "God told me to do thus and thus." If they think God orally gave them such instructions, they need major tranquilizers. Abstain as much as possible from sinful behavior, because sinful behavior causes a lowered self-worth and also grieves God.

When choosing your daily routine, be careful not to overly commit yourself. We choose our own daily routine on the basis of the following list of priorities (but you should decide your own priority list):

(1) Set aside time daily for intimacy with God, including prayer and Scripture meditation.

(2) Set aside time for personal mental health, because you won't be of much use to God, family, or others if you don't have good mental health yourself. This includes time to unwind and relax. It includes time to watch football and other athletic events you may find relaxing. It includes dates with your mate and with other couples for fellowship. It also includes some exercise.

(3) Set aside enough time to be continually building a more

and more intimate relationship with your mate. This includes time for fun, fellowship, serious communication, and a good sex life. Your mate should be an even higher priority than your children.

(4) Set aside enough time to adequately train your children. This includes time to play with them, listen to their problems, pray with them, watch them perform at school, and so forth.

(5) Set aside some of your remaining time to earn a living. The Bible says that if you don't take care of your family's needs, you are worse in God's eyes than an infidel (an atheist). We agree wholeheartedly.

If meeting priorities (1) through (4) means earning less money (and it will for many), then so be it. Your family needs you a thousand times more than they need your money.

(6) With whatever time is left over, develop some ways to use your God-given talents to perform some ministry. Writing books is a ministry we perform bit by bit, during our spare time. Sometimes we go months without writing, because priorities (1) through (5) will not allow it. Don't take on too many jobs at your local church. Pick one function at your church and do it well—for the Lord, not for the approval of men. A few spiritually immature missionaries and pastors have made priority (6) their main priority. As a result, their children, their marriage, their mental health, and, finally, their relationship with and usefulness to God have suffered untold damage. They naively get angry at God for giving them too much to do. God says, "My yoke is easy, and my burden is light." If your work-yoke or spiritual ministry-yoke seems too heavy, take some of it off—it's not from God anyway. It's from your own obsessive-compulsive need to be perfect in order to get the unconscious approval of your father and mother.

7. *Do something nice for one special person each week. This kind deed can be physical (helping with a chore, for example), emotional (buying a book or giving counsel), or spiritual (having devotions together).*

Pray that God will show you ways to help one special person each week. Most Christians are guilty of having *too little introspection*, but then others find insights like those obtained in this book so beneficial that they become overly introspective. This guideline will help you to get more involved in the lives of others. It will help you to realize how useful you really can be. It will show you how significant the little kind things you do for others can be in their lives. It will help you to win the love of others. You will be rewarded for it as well by God. It will also help you to avoid becoming totally wrapped up in introspection or self-pity.

Ask yourself how many of these *"Seven Basic Guidelines"* you are already practicing. Then compare the amount of depression you are experiencing with the amount of happiness you are experiencing. We are certain that you will see a direct relationship. These "Seven Basic Guidelines" will bring happiness, within a few months, to anyone who earnestly (not half-heartedly) puts them into practice. For anyone who personally knows Jesus Christ as his Savior, and lives by these biblical principles, *happiness is a choice*!

13

How Do You Handle Anger?

The third "Guideline for a Happy Life" (chapter 12) was, *Get rid of grudges daily*. Following the principles outlined in this chapter on how to deal with anger will prevent clinical depression from ever developing.

1. *Whenever feeling any significant anger toward yourself, God, or anybody else, you will best handle that anger if you immediately analyze whether it is appropriate or inappropriate. You will thus gain insight into your anger.*

Some of our anger is quite appropriate response (righteous indignation) to someone who has sinned against us.

Examples would include a "friend" spreading gossip or lies about us. Another example is a mate refusing to have sex. According to I Corinthians 7:3-5, a Christian husband and wife should never turn each other down for sex except during prayer. They each have a right to the other's body. If a wife refuses her husband (and the reverse holds true as well), she is violating his God-given right, and it would be appropriate for him to have some righteous indignation (appropriate anger), as long as he forgives her by bedtime (whether she deserves forgiveness or not).

In Ephesians 4:26, we are *commanded* (the Greek verb is in the imperative mood—a command) to "be angry, and sin not." The same verse, however, warns us that we should never let the sun go down on our wrath. We *must not hold grudges*. We must be rid of that dangerous emotion (anger) by sundown (or bedtime). Obviously, if all of our anger were sinful, we would not be commanded by God's Word to "be angry and sin not."

However, much of our anger *is* sinful and inappropriate. There are three main sources of sinful (inappropriate) anger:

(1) *Anger that results when one's selfish demands are not being met*. Selfishness is the root cause of most inappropriate anger. The more selfish a person is (whether he is a criminal who is openly selfish, or a full-time Christian worker who is subtly selfish), the angrier he will be much of the time. He will have serious problems with depression because holding grudges is the main cause of depression.

(2) *Anger that results when one's perfectionistic demands are not being satisfied*. Perfectionists (obsessive-compulsives) expect too much out of themselves, out of others, and even out of God. As a result, they are *frequently* angry toward themselves, others, or God—but mostly toward themselves. They hold grudges against themselves. That's why of all ten personality types which are internationally recognized perfectionists have the highest rate of depression.

(3) *Anger that results from suspiciousness*. When a person has a few paranoid personality traits, he will frequently misinterpret the motives of others. Someone will not notice him, and he will assume that person purposely was avoiding him. Someone will tease him slightly in an attempt to win his friendship, but he will

assume that the "friend" was really cutting him down. A person with paranoid tendencies is so blind to his own repressed anger that he projects it unto others and mistakenly thinks that others are feeling angry toward him. The Bible discusses projection in several places, but especially in Matthew 7:3-5, where Christ himself states:

> And why do you look at the speck in your brother's eye, but do not notice the log that is in your own eye? Or how can you say to your brother, "Let me take the speck out of your eye," and behold, the log is in your own eye? You hypocrite, first take the log out of your own eye; and then you will see clearly enough to take the speck out of your brother's eye.

As we can see from Christ's illustration, sometimes our brother really will have a speck in his eye. But even then we may sometimes blow it out of proportion because of the log in our own. In other words, we may get extremely angry over a minor matter because there is a superabundance of repressed anger in ourselves, or because our brother's sin reminds us of one we ourselves have but are lying to ourselves about. Psychiatrists have long recognized that the type of person we become angry toward the most is probably our own personality type. We humans lie to ourselves so much about our own faults (our blind spots) that whenever someone comes along with similar faults, we find ourselves having a negative basic reaction to him and not understanding why. *All humans do this*, but paranoid personalities are especially so disposed.

In summary, the three main sources of inappropriate anger are (1) *selfishness*, (2) *perfectionistic demands*, and (3) *suspiciousness*.

Anger toward God is always inappropriate, since God claims in Psalm 103 to be perfectly fair (just), righteous (doing what is right), and loving in all that He does. Whenever we feel angry toward God, we should talk to Him about it, realizing that our anger toward God is purely the result of our own human naiveté or selfishness. We must trust God completely to do what is best for us in the long run, instead of being naively angry at Him for not answering a certain prayer *our way*.

It should be obvious by now that gaining insights into the appropriateness or inappropriateness of our anger can be extremely valuable. If we could, through Christian maturity, eliminate most of our inappropriate anger by giving up our selfishness, suspicion, and perfectionistic demands, we would eliminate a majority of our anger.

Gaining insight can also be a tremendous help in overcoming depression. Of course, the first step is for an individual to recognize the fact that he *is angry*. Anger is hard to deal with unless an individual *realizes it is there*. Also, understanding why one becomes so angry in certain situations helps him to control and handle his anger better in the future. For example, perhaps an individual becomes extremely angry when a friend seems to slight him. If he becomes angry out of proportion to the actual event, it may be because the event reminded him of another period in his life when he felt inferior and inadequate. The current event reinforced those past feelings and insecurities. Perhaps 25 percent of his response was to the current situation, and the other 75 percent was his reaction to feelings that were long ago repressed.

Likewise, if an individual can gain insight into his personality he can often learn to control his anger and depression better. For example, if the cyclothymic personality (pp. 205-208) can gain insight into his patterns of behavior, and see how he often sets himself up to get rejected by other people and then becomes angry at them, he can learn to control his inappropriate anger in the future. Also, if the obsessive-compulsive or perfectionistic individual can gain insight into his being overly critical of others (as well as himself), he can learn to control his inappropriate anger in the future. If the hysterical individual can gain insight into the fact that she tends to be overly emotional and becomes very hostile at a moment's notice, the recognition of these patterns can help her control her inappropriate (selfish) anger in the future.

Insight into a person's past life and how it affected him can be a tremendous help in overcoming anger and depression in the present. Likewise, insight into one's current personality traits can be of help in overcoming anger and depression. One word of caution, however: *insight can be dangerous*. If insight is given when a person is not prepared to handle it, it can be dangerous; or if it is given too quickly, it can be dangerous. Some people who gain too much insight too rapidly become psychotic in order to bear the pain of the reality they have learned. In their psychotic state, all their insights are blocked out as they live in unreality. Thus, insight must be given and used with caution, especially in the cases of borderline individuals. Remember to "speak the truth in love."

2. *If you are convinced that your anger is appropriate, you will somehow verbalize that anger and forgive whoever the object of that anger may be by bedtime of the same day. This is in obedience to Matthew 5:21-24 and Ephesians 4:26.*

In Christ's Sermon on the Mount, He gives us the following instructions:

> You have heard that the ancients were told, "You shall not commit murder"; and "Whoever commits murder shall be liable to the court"; but I say to you that every one who is angry with his brother shall be guilty before the court; and whoever shall say to his brother, "Raca [good-for-nothing]," shall be guilty before the supreme court; and whoever shall say, "You fool," shall be guilty enough to go into the hell of fire. If therefore you are presenting your offering at the altar, and there remember that your brother has something against you, leave your offering there before the altar, and go your way; first be reconciled to your brother, and then come and present your offering. (Matthew 5:21-24)

What a fantastic illustration Christ uses here. We humans measure our "superspirituality" by publicly putting a financial offering in a collection plate. But Christ tells us to demonstrate our *genuine spirituality* by loving our brother enough to face up to him, emotional pain and all, and resolve any anger we have toward him or he toward us. Note well that *even if we are not angry toward him, but he is angry toward us, Christ still makes it our responsibility to go to him and reconcile our brother.* That takes great courage and an abundance of Christian maturity and love.

Why does Christ want us to verbalize our anger? There are several psychological and spiritual benefits that come from verbalizing anger:

(1) It helps us to be aware of the truth—that we really are feeling angry—instead of repressing it and wondering why we feel so frustrated or depressed.

(2) It helps us forgive. It is possible to forgive someone without verbalizing our anger, but verbalizing our anger toward him makes forgiving *a great deal easier*, even if the other person does not agree that our anger is appropriate. *We must forgive no matter what response* we get from the other person. Why should *we* suffer depression for *his sin*? That would be foolish. We should verbalize our anger and forgive him whether he deserves forgiveness or not. This will keep us from becoming depressed. God doesn't want us to hold grudges because He wants us to experience love, joy, and peace.

(3) God will use our verbalization, *if done tactfully* (speaking the truth in love), to convict our brother of sin in his life (whatever sin it was that aroused our appropriate anger). *Anger should always be verbalized tactfully. The intent of verbalizing anger should always be to reconcile our brother, never to get vengeance.*

(4) Verbalizing our anger tactfully produces intimacy in a marriage or in a friendship. If we don't verbalize our anger, human nature is such that we will almost certainly end up showing our anger nonverbally through passive (and usually unconscious) games—pouting, procrastinating, burning supper, developing a headache when it's time for sex, coming home late and forgetting to call, and so on.

(5) The person to whom we tactfully verbalize our anger will nearly always *respect* us much more for being (a) assertive, (b) in control of our emotions, and (c) responsible in handling our anger.

(6) Another important benefit from verbalizing our anger tactfully and reconciling our brother is that this is an act of obedience to God's Word.

(7) It helps prevent gossip. If we don't verbalize our anger to the person toward whom we feel anger, the temptation to tell others about how that person has offended us will be almost overwhelming. It will also help keep the other person from gossiping about us by resolving the conflict—or at least bringing the conflict out in the open. It is better to be wounded by a knife than to be mortally wounded by someone's tongue. Several of the seven sins God hates the most (Proverbs 6) involve pride, gossiping, and sowing discord among the brethren. God *hates gossip* but *loves resolution of conflicts*.

A point of clarification is in order before what has been said in this chapter is carried too far. God does not legalistically require each Christian to verbalize every little tidbit of anger he ever feels to every single person toward whom he feels anger. Use your judgment and be practical. For example, you do not try to call the President of the United States if you feel mildly angry about some decision he has made. If you get angry at your boss, and verbalizing your anger would mean losing your job, you may choose to verbalize to God the anger you feel toward your boss, and ask God to help you forgive your boss whether he deserves forgiveness or not. At other times, it might be very appropriate to tactfully share your anger with your boss, or even to write a telegram of protest to the President of the United States concerning one of his decisions. Again, use your judgment and pray for discretion. When angry at your boss, you may find that sharing the problem with your wife later that day will help you bring things into focus and enable you to choose to forgive him. Jogging or hitting a tennis ball can also help you to physically ventilate enough of the anger to bring it into perspective so you can forgive. But though athletics can be a good assistant, be sure never to use athletics as the *only* way to deal with your anger. Even watching contact sports like football can help you symbolically ventilate *part* of your anger. But that is not enough. *You will certainly get depressed* if you hold enough grudges for a long enough time. That old serotonin and norepinephrine will start to get depleted if your "grudge level" remains too high for too long. How high and how long varies with different individuals.

Actually, anger should ideally be ventilated both to God (on a vertical level) and men (on a horizontal level). God is the only one who has supernatural power to deal with our anger. A psychiatrist doesn't, even though he has that magical "M. Deity" degree—at least that's what some patients would like to think M.D. stands for. If you are depressed, pray every night that God will reveal to you any unconscious grudges you may be holding against someone—including yourself. Only God can do that.

This discussion on verbalizing anger would not be complete

without a brief comment about what it means to be *assertive*, as opposed to being *overly aggressive* or *overly passive*. There are two extremes when expressing anger. One is to be aggressive and the other is to be passive. When we are aggressive with our anger, we rid ourselves of our own feelings and vent our own anger at someone else's expense. We attack his character, we attack him personally. The other extreme when expressing anger is to be passive. When we are passive, we do not directly express the way we feel, but we take out our anger in some kind of unconscious passive maneuver such as putting things off, pouting, doing a poor job, letting others run our lives and at the same time resenting it, and saying yes when we really want to say no. Neither extreme is healthy. The healthy balance is found in being assertive. When we are assertive, we do express the way we feel, but we use love and tact in what we say. We say yes when we mean yes and we say no when we mean no. We stand up for what we think we should stand up for, and we ask for what we feel is important. An example may prove helpful. If someone hurt our feelings and we were aggressive, we would attack him personally and attack his character by saying insulting things to him. If we were passive, we would not say anything but simply pout about it (and perhaps talk to others about him behind his back). If we were assertive we would go to him and say something to this effect: "I've been feeling angry about what you said, but I would like for us to resolve our differences. Can we talk about it?"

Remember that no matter how you verbalize your anger, *you must forgive*! Forgiving starts with an *act of the will*. Forgiving is a choice. It may take some time to work through the emotional feelings that are involved. We cannot immediately dismiss the feelings. Again, it takes time to reprogram our computer. It takes time to reprogram the feelings. However, we can forgive others immediately by an *act of the will*. This is an important distinction. It is also important to remember that forgiving does not mean to erase all recall. Rather it means not to charge the offense to someone's account. God the Father forgives us of all of our sins because of what Christ did on the cross for us. This means that He no longer holds our sins against us. He no longer charges them to our account. Logic tells us that if to forgive is to erase all recall, we would all be in trouble. However, to forgive means to impute no longer something to the charge of someone else.

There are basically six groups of people who are often the object of anger and need to be forgiven. First, there is often much repressed anger toward our parents. We need to remember that God can cause difficult situations in the past to work for our advantage, and that for the Christian all things work together for good. We need to remember that we too will make mistakes in raising our children. We need to forgive our parents for mistakes and sins they committed in the past when they were raising us, whether they deserve our forgiveness or not.

Secondly, we need to forgive ourselves. Just as we get angry with other people, we become angry with ourselves for not doing better and making fewer mistakes. We are often critical with ourselves and are harder on ourselves than we are on other people. We need to forgive ourselves for past mistakes and sins. God is aware of our weaknesses. He knows we are but dust (Psalm 103:14). He says that when He removes our sins, they are as far from us as the east is from the west (verse 12). He wants us to do the same and no longer hold our past mistakes against ourselves.

Thirdly, we need to deal with our repressed anger toward God. We do not forgive God, for God has done nothing wrong; but we may have repressed anger or bitter feelings toward Him. We may subconsciously reason in our mind somewhat as follows: "After all, He is God, and He could have prevented or corrected the situation if He had chosen to." Like Job we need to confess our anger toward God, talk with Him about it, and ask Him to help us resolve it.

Fourthly, we need to deal with repressed anger toward our mate. We need to forgive him for mistakes he has made. When two individuals live together for many years, many anger-arousing situations occur, and anger can build up over a period of years and years. An individual needs to forgive in order to prevent depression.

Fifthly, we need to forgive those in authority over us. Anger often builds toward authority figures in our lives. We need to forgive them for whatever wrong we feel they may have done us. God has put them in authority over us. We need to respond to them and learn to talk with them about how we feel. Under no circumstances should we hold grudges against them.

The sixth category of those whom we need to forgive is simply classified as "others." There are often many other people in our lives whom we need to forgive. This group may include our peers when we were young. Various situations may have occurred then, and the repressed feelings and anger were never dealt with. The anger needs to be confessed and the person(s) forgiven.

In the Bible God has said much about anger and the need to control it. One of the best ways we can control anger is to continue to grow in Christ. As we grow in Christ and in humility, much of the anger will automatically dissipate, and thus, we will be happier, healthier individuals.

If, after analyzing your anger, you discover that your anger was inappropriate—the result of your selfishness, perfectionism or suspiciousness—then verbalization of your inappropriate anger will probably not be necessary. However, sometimes it is helpful to verbalize your inappropriate anger. For example:

> Friend, a little while ago I was feeling angry toward you, so I prayed about it and analyzed it. After thinking about it for the past couple of hours, I decided I was letting my perfectionism get out of hand. I was expecting you to be perfect, and started to get upset when you didn't do everything perfectly. Will you forgive me for being so petty? You'll probably have to put up with some pettiness in me if you really want to be my good friend.

As has been discussed earlier, the best way to get rid of inappropriate anger is to give up the sources of inappropriate anger—selfishness, perfectionism, and suspiciousness.

3. *Leave all vengeance up to God. Never get even with anyone, including yourself.*

There is only *one unconscious motive* for retaining anger (for holding grudges): that single motive is *vengeance*. Recently a patient came to our office to gain some insight into his past three years of depression. He was asked if there was anyone he had been especially angry with three years ago, that is, just prior to developing his depression. Though initially surprised at the question, after thinking about it for less than a minute he appeared to be getting angry. His neck was getting blotchy and red, his pupils began to dilate, and his fingers began to subtly draw into a fist. He used many curse words to describe a teacher who, three years ago, in front of his college peers, had accused him of cheating, even though he hadn't cheated. He described the incident with vivid hostility. When asked, "Why don't you forgive your teacher? It will help you get over your depression," he replied angrily, "Absolutely not! I'll never forgive her till the day I die. She doesn't deserve it!" At that point it seemed appropriate to gently poke fun at the patient, to help him see the absurdity of his position: "You're really punishing her, aren't you! You're going through three years of depression to get vengeance on her. Is it worth it? Do you think she even remembers who you are?" The mechanisms of depression were explained to him—how biochemical changes are brought on by holding grudges. Here was also a marvelous opportunity to share Christ with him. After developing a relationship with Christ, and using Christ's power to help him forgive his teacher—even though she really didn't deserve forgiveness—he got over his depression in a matter of weeks after suffering from its symptoms for three years.

Vengeance is a stupid motive. If you have any faith in God, personal vengeance is totally unnecessary and stupid. God will wreak vengeance on all who deserve it—or else He will show His divine grace and forgive them, especially if they have repented. But whether God shows vengeance or divine grace, it's God's decision. It's none of your business. Stay out of God's business! We humans spend half our lives trying to play God in various ways. We are so ignorant! Of course it is a good thing that we are at least a little smarter than the animals. But even though we are a little smarter than the animals, only man gets himself so depressed that he kills himself.

Let's look at what the apostle Paul said about vengeance in Romans 12:17-21:

> Never pay back evil for evil to anyone. Respect what is right

> in the sight of all men. If possible, so far as it depends on you, be at peace with all men.
>
> Never take your own revenge, beloved, but leave room for the wrath of God, for it is written,
>
> *"Vengeance is mine, I will repay, says the Lord. But if your enemy is hungry, feed him, and if he is thirsty, give him a drink: for in so doing you will heap burning coals upon his head."*
>
> Do not be overcome by evil, but overcome evil with good.

God's Word is so beautiful. His ways are so wise. If we proud humans would only listen! If we would only forgive others when they wrong us, and forgive ourselves when we make mistakes, we would never suffer the pains of depression.

In summary, there are three major principles for dealing with anger: (1) Gain insight into whether your anger is appropriate or inappropriate; (2) *Verbalize* your significant, appropriate anger, and *forgive* before bedtime; (3) Never get vengeance on anyone—leave that to God.

It is our hope that thousands will put these principles into practice. *Happiness is a choice*, but the only path to happiness is God's path, as outlined in His Word.

14

When Are Medication and Hospitalization Advantageous?

Should antidepressant medications ever be used? There are some Christians who would say no. They would say it is unspiritual to rely on medications at all since we should rely totally on the Lord. A century ago, a number of Christians thought it was a sin to wear glasses—or "devil's eyes," as they called them. Their reasoning was, "If God wanted you to be able to see, He would have given you good vision." Even after penicillin was discovered, many Christians died of pneumonia because they wanted to trust God alone and not medications. We know of several Christians who have died in the past few years because they refused to have a cancer surgically removed. Instead, they believed some fanatical evangelists who told them they were miraculously healed. The president of the student body of a major university died of cancer in 1977 after personally convincing his state government to legalize Laetrile—the highly dubious drug to which he attributed his "healing."

Technically, mankind has come a long way; he has even walked on the moon. But when it comes to common sense, whether it be Christians or non-Christians, we have not advanced a great deal from where we were during the Dark Ages.

Christ Himself said that those who are sick need a physician. Luke, who wrote a larger quantity of the New Testament (including Acts) than did the apostle Paul, was a physician. Just because God used numerous miracles in the early church to prove that Christianity was true (prior to the Scriptures being completed), does that justify the insistence of twentieth-century Christians that God heal them supernaturally or not at all? It takes a grandiose person to *demand* a supernatural healing. God certainly does heal some people supernaturally on rare occasions today, but He heals most Christians through the common-sense application of medical technology and medications. Why did He give man a brain if He never expected him to use it? Should Christian diabetics who need insulin daily use insulin? Or should they refuse insulin and die in diabetic coma within two days in order to prove how brave and superspiritual they are? Well, all we can say is, you can die for your superspirituality if you choose to, but we choose to live. We choose to live totally for Christ, but we also choose to believe He wants us to use the common sense He gave us. We also choose happiness over depression.

Should antidepressants ever be used? Of course, under certain circumstances.[1] When a patient comes to us and is clinically depressed, cannot sleep, and has suicidal ideation, we have three ways in which we could treat him. We could see him in weekly therapy with no medications, and he would be totally over his clinical depression within six to twelve months on the average (that is, if he doesn't commit suicide during those first two months when he continues to suffer insomnia and be in severe emotional pain). A second option would be for that same patient to come for weekly psychotherapy and take antidepressants, in which case he would probably be totally over his depression in three to six months. He would be sleeping well and feeling some improvement after his first ten days on antidepressant medications, so suicide would be less of a risk. A third option is for that same patient to check himself into the psychiatry ward of a general hospital, get daily psychotherapy and medication, feel better within a week, and be totally over his depression within three to six weeks, requiring only a month or two of follow-up outpatient psychotherapy. Which option is the most spiritual if the patient has four children at home who have been hurting for months because of his depression? Which option is the most spiritual if suicide is a real possibility, a possibility that would leave children fatherless (or motherless) and with deep emotional scars?

Our opinion is that if the depressed individual is either a suicide risk or near the point where he may break with reality (a psychotic depression), then hospitalization is almost a must. Why take chances with a human life? If the individual is so depressed he is not functioning well, but he is neither suicidal nor on the verge of a break with reality, then outpatient psychotherapy with medication is the best choice. Why should a patient spend an extra three to six months being depressed just so he can brag that he didn't use medication? For mild depressions, it is better not to use medications, since medications are expensive and have mild temporary side effects, such as dryness of the mouth and a slower reaction time when one is driving.

The advantages of hospitalization for treatment of severe depressions can be summarized as follows:

1. The patient receives intensive psychotherapy.
2. Adjustments in medications can be made rapidly.
3. The patient gets away from his stressful environment into a safe retreat.
4. He is protected by hospital precautions from suicide attempts.
5. There is a friendly, helpful, supportive atmosphere.
6. Becoming acquainted with other depressed individuals who are getting better is a source of encouragement.

7. The symptoms and emotional pain of depression are more rapidly cured.
8. Trained psychiatric nurses and other staff members assist psychiatric physicians in counseling and helping patients gain insights.
9. Nurses observe the daily behavior patterns of patients and relay this information to psychiatrists who can use it to help patients gain insights.
10. Hospitalization is usually less expensive (in the long run) to the individual than is prolonged outpatient psychotherapy since it is generally covered by insurance. Also the patient is frequently able to return to full employment more rapidly.

The disadvantages of hospitalization are:

1. Some dependent individuals try to escape responsibility by getting themselves admitted to a hospital and feigning the symptoms of depression when the psychiatrist is around.
2. There is some social stigma attached to a psychiatric hospitalization, especially among the lower and lower-middle classes. It could hinder some job promotions and could even prevent getting some jobs.
3. When the patient is discharged three to six weeks after being admitted, he (or she) is now happy, enthusiastic, and over the bulk of the depression, but finds that his friends are hesitant at first to ask him questions about his hospitalization for fear of hurting his feelings. The patient may take this personally as a rejection, even though it isn't.
4. Without insurance, hospitalization is very costly, averaging nearly $1,000 per week total cost in 1978. Even with insurance, it is not ethical to run up high hospital bills unless it is considered necessary.

We never use insulin coma therapy or electroconvulsive therapy (also called ECT, EST, or "Shock" Therapy), because there is some potential risk to the patient and because these measures bring only temporary relief in many cases. Shock therapy may cure a present depression but does not teach the individual how to prevent getting depressed again. Some Christian psychiatrists do use shock therapy for suicidal patients or patients who are resistant to antidepressant medications and do not seem to be improving. They generally follow up the shock therapy with outpatient psychotherapy.

We also do not believe in using addicting medications. Tricyclic antidepressants, such as Tofranil, Elavil, and Sinequan, are not addicting. They are taken in doses of about 150 milligrams at bedtime daily, generally for three to six months. After that, if the conflicts are resolved and the person's norepinephrine levels are restored to normal, he can stop taking the antidepressants and feel just as happy without them as he did when taking them.

Many other topics related to drugs and treatment could be discussed here. However, we have deferred discussion of the more technical topics to Appendix 3.

15

How Do You Handle Anxiety?

In Luke 8:14 are listed three obstacles that choke individuals after they hear the Word of God. Two of these (the pleasures of this life and riches) most of us heard about when we were growing up, but how many heard about the third (care or anxieties)? Truly, anxieties choke many people. And yet all of us have some anxiety at times.

Anxiety often accompanies depression. It is an emotion which is characterized by feelings of uneasiness, apprehension, dread, concern, tension, restlessness, and worry.

The anxious individual often anticipates misfortune, danger, or doom.

Symptoms of Anxiety

The anxious individual may be hyperalert, irritable, fidgety and overdependent. He may talk too much and have difficulty falling asleep. His concentration may be impaired and his memory poor. He may be immobilized by his anxiety.

The anxious individual may experience excessive perspiration, muscle tension, headaches, a quivering voice, sighing respirations, episodes of hyperventilation, abdominal pain, nausea, diarrhea, "butterflies" in his stomach, high blood pressure, a rapid heartbeat, fainting episodes, frequent urination, impotence, or frigidity.

Anxiety is the underlying cause of most psychiatric problems. It is the cause of neuroses, psychoses, and psychophysiologic disorders. It is the cause of phobias. It can be the real underlying problem in people who think they have committed the unpardonable sin.

Both psychology and the Scriptures point to the fact that anxiety can be either normal or abnormal. Psychologists have long noted that individuals are more efficient and productive when they have some anxiety. However, if the anxiety becomes intense, their efficiency begins to decrease accordingly.

The Scriptures also indicate that some anxiety (a realistic concern as seen in such verses as I Corinthians 12:25; II Corinthians 11:28; Philippians 2:20) is healthy. However, intense anxiety (fretting and worrying, as seen in Luke 8:14; Philippians 4:6; I Peter 5:7) is not healthy.[1] The Greek word often translated "anxiety" is used about twenty-five times in the New Testament.[2] It is usually used in the negative sense (implying worrying or fretting), but occasionally in the positive sense (a realistic concern).

Technically, anxiety is secondary to unconscious conflicts while fear is secondary to conscious conflicts. However, practically speaking, the two can often not be separated. There are approximately 350 passages in the Bible that tell us to "fear not."

Causes of Anxiety

The causes of anxiety are many. It can be the result of unconscious intrapsychic conflicts. It can be learned by example—such as identifying with parents who are anxious. It can come from childhood conflicts. It can come from present-day situational problems. It can come from being anxious about being anxious. It can come from fears of inferiority, poverty, or poor health.

In early childhood all of us have experiences that create anxiety. When an individual has a particularly stressful childhood with many bad experiences, he suffers a great deal of anxiety. Much of this anxiety is not dealt with at the time it appears, but is repressed into the subconscious instead. Earlier in this book mention was made of Penfield, the neurosurgeon who found that the brain functions in much the same manner as a high-fidelity tape recorder. It functions, so to speak, like a computer with memory banks. Penfield found that when he touched certain areas of the brain with electrodes, an individual would sometimes remember specific events, sometimes he would also remember the feeling that occurred with those events, and sometimes he would just recall a feeling, such as elation or depression, without any specific recollection of the event. From this, Penfield concluded that specific memories and emotions are recorded and stored, and that they can be replayed today in as vivid a form as when they occurred. They are aroused by current-day stress. When an individual encounters current-day situations and experiences that cause anxiety, his anxiety from his early childhood is also aroused. In most cases it is the emotions from childhood which are aroused—the specific event is usually not recalled. The repressed emotions seem to apply to the current day, although they really do not—at least, not in the proportion to which they are being experienced. This explains why we often overreact to current-day situations. We are reacting not only to the current-day stresses, but also to the repressed emotions of childhood. Anxiety from the current situation then may also be partially repressed into the subconscious. It may even be displaced into an obsessive worry or a phobia. Also, it may be internalized, resulting in depression. Additional anxiety may be created as the individual becomes anxious over being anxious, or as he develops anxiety over the particular phobia or obsession that he has, or as he develops anxiety over being depressed.

Ten Behavior Patterns and Attitudes Taken from Scripture that Will Decrease Anxiety

Philippians 4 prescribes ten ways in which to overcome anxiety:

1. Determine to obey God. God commands us not to be anxious (Philippians 4:5).
2. Pray (Philippians 4:6). God told Daniel not to fear because God had heard his prayer from the time he first started praying and *He would answer* (Daniel 10:12).
3. Realize that God can keep our mind safe as we obey Him (Philippians 4:7).
4. Meditate on positive thoughts (Philippians 4:8). We have often encouraged people who catch themselves worrying to say, "Stop, relax; anxiety is a signal to relax, so relax." We then encourage them to go over and over a verse like Philippians 4:8. Anxiety is usually a signal to become more anxious, but by a simple technique of behavior modification the brain can be conditioned to use anxiety as a signal to relax. There is no better place to find positive things to meditate on than the Scriptures (Psalm 34:4; 86:15; Proverbs 1:33; 3:25, 26; Isaiah 40:28-31; Matthew 6:33, 34; 11:28-30; John 10:27, 28; 14:27; II Corinthians 11:3; Hebrews 4:15; I John 3:20; 4:10).
5. Focus on godly behavior (Philippians 4:9). We often tell anxious individuals to avoid sin (Proverbs 4:15), and to join small fellowship groups (Hebrews 10:24, 25).
6. Divert attention from self to others (Philippians 4:10; see also Philippians 2:3, 4). As an individual gets his mind off his own problems by helping others, his anxiety often decreases.
7. Work on being content (Philippians 4:11; see also I Timothy 6:6).
8. Realize there is a twofold responsibility (yours and Christ's) in doing anything. "I can do all things through Christ. . ." (Philippians 4:13). An individual can overcome anxiety through Christ.
9. Eliminate the fear of poverty (Philippians 4:19). God promises to supply all our needs (not all our wants).

10. Realize that the grace of God is with you (Philippians 4:23; see also II Corinthians 9:8).

In addition to the ways for overcoming anxiety that are taught in Philippians are these that are suggested by common sense:

1. Listen to Christian music (I Samuel 16:23).
2. Get adequate exercise—ideally three times per week.
3. Get adequate sleep (Psalm 127:2). Most people need eight hours of sleep per night.
4. Do what you can to deal with the fear or problem causing the anxiety. Examine different alternatives or possible solutions and try one.
5. Talk with a close friend at least once a week about your frustrations.
6. Get adequate recreation—ideally two to three times per week.
7. Live one day at a time (Matthew 6:34). Probably 98 percent of the things we are anxious about or worry about never happen. Learning to live one day at a time is an art that can be cultivated.
8. Imagine the worst thing that could possibly happen. Then consider why that wouldn't be so bad after all.
9. Don't put things off. Putting things off causes more anxiety.
10. Set a time limit on your worries.

Many individuals have been programmed all their lives to worry about something. One way to stop reinforcing bad programming is to limit the amount of time spent each day in worrying. Many individuals worry every moment of every day. Their life is one of constant misery and they are continuously in emotional pain. We have found a very simple (yet seemingly profound) technique that has helped many of these individuals. We encourage them to set aside a definite period of time each day, such as fifteen minutes in the evening, to consider and ponder whatever their particular problem might be. Then, anytime during the day when the issue comes to their mind, they simply say to themselves, "Self, I cannot consider that issue right now. I will consider it later during the designated time period, but I refuse to consider it at this moment." By doing this they set free much of the mental energy that would otherwise be wasted in worry and that would also reinforce their bad programming and add to their depressive mood. These individuals have been wasting many hours worrying about things, most of which will never happen. Probably 98 percent of the things we worry about never come true. In Matthew 6 we are exhorted *not to worry* about future events, and to handle but one day at a time. Christ states that each day has enough trouble of its own without borrowing from the future. Worrying is a choice, since the apostle Paul commands us to "be anxious for nothing." In summary, we need to live one day at a time and, if worries continue to intrude into consciousness, to use the simple technique of putting time aside, a limited time, for pondering the issue. This will help us to regulate ourselves. Then we won't worry about the problem all day long and utilize all our mental energy to reinforce our anxiety, depression, and negative thinking.

16

How Do You Find Lifelong Happiness?

A concerned father and mother
had a child whom they loved very much.
The parents showed much love and warmth,
and communicated with their child on a very
deep and intense level.
The parents taught their only child
everything they thought might help
prepare him for the future.
When it was necessary, they rebuked and
disciplined their beloved child. When
it came time for moving away from the nest
to establish an independent life, the
parents had mixed emotions: love, hope,
confidence—and apprehension.

It is with these emotions that we write
the final chapter to you, the reader.
We feel love for you,

even though we do not know you personally. We hope you will choose happiness for life. We are confident that you will obtain it if you live by the principles of God instead of the naive principles of this pagan world. We will be praying for you and for the continued ministry of this book. And yet we feel enough apprehension to write for you this final chapter, in much the same manner as the parents of the beloved child apprehensively give him some final warnings about life as he steps out into the world on his own. This chapter is a list of final tidbits of advice for you to apply on your road to happiness.

1. *Change the way you talk to yourself*. All of us go through each day "talking to ourselves" in our thoughts. We talk either in a positive tone or a negative, critical tone. If we constantly criticize ourselves, we will undoubtedly hold grudges against ourselves and get depressed. Quit condemning yourself. Look at the positive things in your life. Look at your accomplishments instead of dwelling on past failures. Would you ever criticize another person as much as you subconsciously criticize yourself? You may think you need all that harsh talk, but you don't—so get off your back!

2. *Understand your feelings, but focus on behavior*. You don't do what you do because you feel the way you feel—you feel the way you feel because you do what you do. Think about that for a moment. In other words, your actions (godly actions or ungodly actions) will determine how you feel. If you choose to love your mate, for example, and choose to act lovingly and respectfully toward your mate, the feeling of love will follow whether it was there before or not.

Therapists have often tended to go to one extreme or the other in dealing with people's feelings versus their behavior. Some therapists (such as psychoanalysts) emphasize feelings, whereas others (such as therapists from the schools of behavior modification or reality therapy) emphasize behavior. We believe *both* should be dealt with. First of all, feelings are important and should be dealt with. The writer of Hebrews noted that Christ could be touched with the feelings of our infirmities. Christ does understand our feelings, and He does care when we hurt. It is important to have insight into our feelings and deal with our feelings. It is important to understand how events in our early life may influence the way we feel now. It is important that we have the freedom to share our feelings and problems with those we love. Thus, feelings are very important.

However, we should not let our feelings rule our lives. Many, many times in the Scriptures the emphasis is on what we do. For example, Philippians 4:13 says, "I can do all things through Christ who strengtheneth me." In Philippians 2:13 the apostle Paul states, "For it is God who worketh in you both to will and to do of his good pleasure." In Matthew 7:24-27 Christ states:

> Therefore, whosoever heareth these sayings of mine, and doeth them, I will liken him unto a wise man, who built his house upon a rock. And the rain descended, and the floods came, and the winds blew and beat upon that house, and it fell not; for it was founded upon a rock. And every one that heareth these sayings of mine, and doeth them not, shall be likened unto a foolish man, who built his house upon the sand. And the rain descended, and the floods came, and the winds blew and beat upon that house and it fell; and great was the fall of it.

This is a comparison of a stable individual and an unstable individual. We note that both of them have trials and tribulations. On both houses the rain descended, the floods came, and the wind blew; but one was able to endure *because of what he did* whereas the other was not.

Moreover, we have very little direct control over our emotions, but we have maximum control over our behavior. In other words, we can change our feelings with our will only to a certain degree, whereas our behavior is under the complete and maximum control of our will. In Genesis 4:6, 7, Moses recorded, "And the Lord said unto Cain, Why art thou angry? And why is thy countenance fallen? If thou doest well, shalt thou not be accepted? And if thou doest not well, sin lieth at the door. And unto thee shall be his desire, and thou shalt rule over him." In this passage the Lord refers to feelings; in fact, He refers to anger, and to a fallen countenance (which is indicative of depression). And then He goes on to say that feelings can be changed by changing behavior. He states in effect, "If you do well, will not your countenance be lifted up?" This is a cycle—one follows the other—how we feel does tend to affect what we do, but it is also true that what we do can change the way we feel. Since we have minimal control over our feelings, we should focus on our behavior. We have had many housewives say to us, "I am going to begin to get up in the morning and to start doing something, that is, if I ever feel like it, or if this depression ever lifts." At that point we think to ourselves, "Oh, no; what if she never feels like it!" In that case she has just doomed herself to a life of misery.

In summary, we need to understand our feelings; we need to find a friend to talk with about our feelings and to deal with those feelings. However, at that point, we need to go beyond feelings and focus on behavior. While our feelings should be understood, they should not run our lives, because feelings are very fickle and subject to change. They can change like the ocean tide; they can rise and fall just as quickly. A much more stable focus on which to base our lives is *behavior*. We should determine to ground our behavior in sound logic and firm biblical convictions.

3. *Focus on a specific plan of action*. In overcoming depression, one needs to go beyond saying to himself, "I need to change my behavior." He needs to figure out a specific plan of action for changing that behavior. It is the little things we do in our day-to-day activities that determine how we feel. It is the little things—such as the time we get up in the morning, our first response to our mate in the morning, whether or not we eat breakfast, whether or not we have some quiet time with the Lord, whether or not we have a verse that we are thinking about for encouragement during that day, whether or not we are overloaded in our work, whether or not we are having enough social contact, whether or not we are eating a good diet, whether or not we are having regular exercise—these things determine how we feel. This may seem so simple, but many, many individuals improve by forcing themselves to figure out a specific plan of action consisting of perhaps ten things they are going to do daily for the next week. After they have worked on the schedule they have developed for perhaps a month or two,

almost invariably there is noticeable improvement.

Take the case of a patient who was considering suicide. In the emergency room, when asked what was going on and what was troubling him, he stated that when he awoke that morning he had felt depressed, and because he felt depressed, he decided not to go to work. Then he felt depressed about not going to work. He started watching television, and some soap operas came on. He started to identify with the soap operas, and then he really got depressed. (It's a wonder he wasn't even more depressed!) When asked if he might be doing something that he thought was wrong, something which could be intensifying his depression, he said he was doing one thing in particular that made him feel very guilty and intensified his depression. When this individual was given help to change his behavior, he became happier. The little things that we do in our day-to-day life do determine how we feel.

Or take the case of a housewife who was very depressed. Asked to outline her daily schedule, she stated that she slept late in the mornings because she felt so depressed she did not want to get up. Of course, she then felt depressed about sleeping late. She also was not cooking her husband's breakfast. This was something she felt that she ought to do, and she felt depressed about not doing it. Making very specific plans to change her daily activities enabled her to overcome her depression. The list of things that she planned to do to help her overcome her depression included: (1) Get up early at least three mornings out of seven regardless of how you feel; (2) every week memorize one verse on depression; (3) have more social contact; (4) do certain activities around the house that you ought to do and will make you feel better for having done them. By changing her activity and by ventilating her feelings, she was able to overcome her depression.

If individuals feel depressed about a certain situation, we suggest that they sit down and list the different options they have and things they can do to overcome depression. Then they need to implement the plan and to commit themselves to their plan for at least a week at a time. If after a few weeks their plan is not working, we suggest making a new plan, and trying some new options. But they must get off dead center! Many individuals think that when they are facing a particular problem that is causing them to be depressed, there are no other options—that there are no other things they can try. However, if they will sit down and make a list of all the options—the probable options, the possible options, and even the ridiculous options—they will often be surprised at how many they can come up with. By reserving evaluation of the options until they are all listed, the process of creativity will not be hindered. Sometimes, one of the ridiculous options will turn out to be one that may be quite practical and that they will use.

In summary, if one is depressed, he should implement a specific plan of action for overcoming his depression. He should commit himself to this plan, and work on it from day to day for a period of several weeks. Usually he will begin to see improvement.

4. *Develop new interests and activities*. The depressed individual often gets in a rut. He will benefit by developing new interests and new activities. He may need to go to a movie with his wife. He may need merely to drive home a different way. He may need to develop some new friendships. He may benefit from getting involved in some athletic activity. Depressed individuals will benefit if they will force themselves to develop new interests and new activities. Again, the results of this will not be seen immediately, but over a period of several weeks depressed individuals usually will begin to feel better.

5. *Utilize the resource of prayer.* The benefits of prayer in cases of depression were mentioned briefly above. A little amplification at this point should prove beneficial, since prayer is a tremendous resource at the disposal of depressed individuals. Through prayer we can incorporate supernatural strength. Through prayer we can call upon supernatural powers to help us in our depression. Prayer is more than positive thinking; it is more than the power of suggestion; and it is more than magical thinking, which some psychiatrists would call it. It is calling upon the power of God Himself who is available to His children. In I John 5:14, 15, we read: "And this is the confidence that we have in him, that, if we ask any thing according to his will, he

heareth us; and if we know that he hears us, whatever we ask, we know that we have the petitions that we desired of him." God does not want us to be depressed; He wants us to call upon Him so that He can help us to overcome our depression. James said that " [we] have not because [we] ask not" (4:2). James also recorded that Elias was a man "subject to like passions as we are," and that "he prayed earnestly that it might not rain, and it rained not." Elias was a man subject to like passions as we are, and yet God honored his prayer. God will honor our prayers today and help us to overcome our depression. In John 15:7, Christ promises that if we abide in Him, we shall ask whatsoever we will, and it shall be done unto us. The men who count the most for God are men who spend time every day in prayer. Both Martin Luther and John Wesley spent several hours every day in prayer. In Ephesians 6 the apostle Paul tells of the spiritual warfare in which we are engaged. Satan likes nothing better than to have Christians become depressed and no longer effective for Christ. Through a depression, Satan can render a Christian as noneffective as if he had committed adultery or some other gross sin. Also in that same chapter, the apostle Paul encourages his fellow Christians to pray.

6. *Utilize the resource of the Word of God*. The tremendous resource that we have available through the Word of God was already mentioned briefly, but further amplification of this point may prove helpful. The Word of God has tremendous power—power for many things, including overcoming depression. In the Old and New Testament, it is recorded over forty times that the world was created by the word of God. In Hebrews 11:3 it is recorded that through faith we understand that the worlds were framed by the word of God. We understand this verse to mean that the worlds were created simply by the word of God. God simply spoke His word and created the universe. Now that is astounding when one considers how large the universe is. If one were to travel at the speed of light and to cross our Milky Way alone, which is only one galaxy of many billions and billions of galaxies, he would be a hundred thousand years old before completing his journey.[1] This is almost beyond the human comprehension. If God's spoken word can do that, then surely

His written Word can help to overcome depression in the individual's life.

Concerning the Word of God we read in II Peter 1:4: "By which are given unto us exceedingly great and precious promises, that by these ye might be partakers of the divine nature, having escaped the corruption that is in the world through lust." By God's promises in His Word, we can be partakers of His divine nature. How much more stable can one be than to be a partaker of God's divine nature? That should be able to effect tremendous stability in our lives. Peter tells us here that through the Word we are able to escape lust, and in another passage (I Peter 2:11), he tells us that lust could destroy our souls (or our minds, emotions, and will). In other words, lust can make us weak emotionally and more prone to emotional problems such as depression. But through the Word of God, we can overcome. Through the Word of God we can become stable and strong. The key to changing our lives and to overcoming our problems through the Word of God lies in our loving, studying, and meditating upon the Word. Nothing can help more in overcoming life's problems than spending hours and hours meditating upon the Word of God. Initially one might memorize Scripture verses to help overcome problems, but through the years, he will grow to love the Word. Jeremiah the prophet noted that God's words were found, and he did eat them, and they were the joy and rejoicing of his heart (15:16).

The Bible is more than a book to be studied; it is a book that needs to be applied. We need to spend some time every day studying the Word, memorizing the Word, and then considering, "How can I apply that to my life today?" For example, when the Bible says to be anxious for nothing, we need to think, "Now Lord, what does that mean? How can I go about today being anxious for nothing? What are some practical ways that I can do that? I pray for your divine help and guidance."

Individuals want freedom from their depression. This freedom can come through the Word of God. Christ said, "And ye shall know the truth, and the truth shall make you free." His Word can free us from anything—even depression.

7. *Develop a friendship*. Most people who are severely depressed feel they do not have a single friend to whom they can

talk. They often have no one with whom they can just be themselves. They intensely fear rejection. Simply developing a friendship can be of great assistance in overcoming depression. In Ecclesiastes 4:9, 10, Solomon says: "Two are better than one, because they have a good reward for their labor; For if they fall, the one will lift up his fellow. But woe to him that is alone when he falleth; for he hath not another to help him up." We note here that in our struggles through life, we need a friend. This passage uses the phrase, "if they fall." However, when a person is alone in life, it is not a matter of *if* he falls, but a matter of *when*. In Psalm 142:4 David exclaims, "I looked on my right hand, and beheld, but there was no man that would know me. Refuge failed me; no man cared for my soul." We need friends that we can go to—friends who watch over our souls, to whom we can bare our hearts, and by whom we know we will be accepted.

Being alone can cause depression, or it can certainly reinforce a depression already present. During World War II, the enemy conducted experiments to find the most effective type of punishment. They found that the most effective type of punishment was solitary confinement. After a few days in solitary confinement, most men would tell all. Individuals that do not have enough water hallucinate about water, and individuals that are kept in solitary confinement hallucinate about people. We need people, and we need friends. This can be of major importance in overcoming depression. Individuals who fail, on the other hand, often feel no one truly loves them on an unconditional basis. In Hebrews 4, the author relates to us that one way to keep from being hardened by the deceitfulness of sin is to be exhorted by another Christian.

A friend is someone who is warm, concerned, caring, and open in sharing the problems he has had and how he has overcome them. He is sensitive, loving, and accepting. A friend is one who is willing to give of himself to another. In I Thessalonians 2:8 Paul says, "So, being affectionately desirous of you, we were willing to have imparted unto you, not the gospel of God only, but also our own souls, because ye were dear unto us." A friend is one who really cares when we hurt. Note again the words of the apostle Paul: "My little children, of whom I travail in birth again until Christ be formed in you . . ." (Galatians

4:19). Paul really cared when others were hurting. It must have been a real encouragement to them that someone loved them and prayed for them that much.

Many of us have experienced a great relief from depression when a friend sat down to listen to us and to give us some support and guidance. It is difficult for a depressed individual to develop friendships because he cannot understand how anyone could care for him. He fears rejection. He fears that if he really gets close, he will be rejected. As he is able to overcome this frame of mind and begins to develop friendships, he finds that this thinking is inaccurate, and that these friendships can help him to overcome his depression.

Because depressives are afraid to become close to others they may develop defense mechanisms whereby they keep others at a distance. These defenses are usually of four major types: denial, displacement, introjection, and projection.[2]

First, they use denial. They may deny their need for others. In other words, they deny their own dependency needs. They may cover up these needs by helping others. They may have a large number of superficial friends, but none who are really close. They use the technique of denial to avoid getting really close to others.

Secondly, as the depressive denies his own dependency needs, he also denies that he is anxious and angry because these dependency needs are not being met. He displaces his anxiety onto his body and may develop physical problems such as peptic ulcer.

Thirdly, the depressive uses the defense mechanism of introjection whereby he assumes blame for things he didn't do. He accepts responsibility for events which, realistically, are outside of his control. One counselee said he felt guilty when he saw his boss having an affair with a young lady. This defense has been said to have its genesis in man's need to feel important. The depressive can't really be the nobody he feels he is if he is so guilty, so responsible. The depressive uses his introjection combined with projection to keep himself at a distance from other people.

Projection is the opposite of introjection in many ways. The projector assigns to others his own faults and feelings. If the depressive doesn't want to get close to others (for fear of getting rejected), he might project his feelings onto them and feel they don't want to get close to him. He might feel they are standoffish.

The depressive uses these four defenses to severely distort communication and to keep others at a distance.

8. *Grow in fellowship*. Not only can a depressed individual benefit from developing friendships with specific individuals, but he can also benefit tremendously from the body of Christ as a whole. Most of the biblical epistles were not written to individuals but to a body of believers. Much of the language used in the Bible pertains to the whole body and not merely to certain individuals. In Ephesians 4:14-18 Paul records:

> That we henceforth be no more children, tossed to and fro, and carried about with every wind of doctrine, by the sleight of men, and cunning craftiness, by which they lie in wait to deceive; But, speaking the truth in love, may grow up into him in all things, who is the head, even Christ; From whom the whole body fitly joined together and compacted by that which every joint supplieth, according to the effectual working in the measure of every part, maketh increase of the body unto the edifying of itself in love. This I say, therefore, and testify in the Lord, that ye henceforth walk not as other Gentiles walk, in the vanity of their mind.

There is real protection among and within the body of Christ. If we are with a group of believers that love the Lord and enjoy life, their happiness rubs off on us. We find ourselves being less self-centered and less absorbed in our own problems. We find our depression lifting. Of course, involvement in group activities with other believers is contrary to what the depressive initially wants to do for he wants to withdraw and be alone. However, withdrawing and being alone is the worst thing he can do, for withdrawing reinforces his depression.

9. *Realize no one is perfect*. The depressed individual needs to realize that no one is perfect and that everyone makes mistakes and does sin from time to time. The depressed individual is unduly hard on himself, unwilling to forgive himself, and makes unrealistic demands upon himself. He doesn't allow

himself to make any mistakes. He is a hard taskmaster. In I John 1:8 is recorded: "If we say that we have no sin, we deceive ourselves and the truth is not in us." Again, we need to realize that no one is perfect, that all of us sin, and that we all make mistakes. We need to understand that we can benefit from our mistakes and learn from them. The depressed individual needs to realize that no one is perfect. He needs to lower his unrealistic expectations of himself.

10. *Focus on assertiveness*. The depressed individual is often very nonassertive. It is obvious that it is wrong to be aggressive, to run over other people and hurt them unnecessarily. However, it is also wrong to be passive—not to speak up when we ought to speak up, but rather to internalize our feelings and become bitter. A depressed individual tends to become passive. He lets others run over him. He simply takes it and turns inward, becoming bitter and depressed. Depressive individuals may be passive for a long time and let their anger build and build and build, until eventually they go to the other extreme and explode in some aggressive behavior. The healthy balance is to be assertive. To be assertive is to express in love and in a tactful way how we feel. To be assertive is to keep others from being irresponsible, especially when it concerns us and relates to us. Generally having gone too far in being passive, depressed individuals need to work on being more assertive.

11. *Deal with dependency needs*. Depressed individuals often have many dependency needs.[3] However, they do not know how to take care of their dependency needs in a healthy way. They ought to get close to others since this would help fulfill their dependency needs. However, because they fear rejection, they do not get close, and thus, their dependency needs increase all the more. They may try to deal with their dependency needs by going to the opposite extreme and becoming very independent. They may become a "super person" and a helper of others. It has been noted that they not only need no one, but they can help all.[4] Of course, this is a defense mechanism whereby they deny their own needs and try to compensate by becoming helpers of others. However, the basic problem of their underlying

depression still remains and complicates their lives. They need to learn to deal with these dependency needs by going ahead and taking a chance on getting close to others. They may have to change some patterns in their life to do this. For example, they may need to stop a life pattern of rejecting others because they fear they might get rejected. They can learn that they can get close to others by simply no longer rejecting them. Individuals may have put on excess weight to keep other people from getting close. They need to learn that it is safe to lose the weight and to go ahead and get close to others. They may need to deal with an alcohol problem; some may be abusing alcohol in order to keep others at a distance. They have numbed their brain so they cannot be hurt by others. Again, they need to learn they can get close in a healthy way, and they will not always be hurt. They may need to change a pattern of compensation by means of which they have come to think of themselves as superhuman. This being a superhuman may be of some temporary help but it usually soon adds to depression because dependency needs are being met less and less. This pattern needs to be changed. This is not to say that those who fall into this pattern should stop helping others. Rather they should realize what they are doing and get their lives more in balance.

12. *Recognize fear of rejection*. Depressed individuals are often caught up in a very unhealthy cycle. They have excessive needs from within. They have many dependency needs that were not met in their childhood; these dependency needs are still present and crave attention. However, while they have many dependency needs, they have learned to expect people to fall short, perhaps just as their parents fell short and did not meet their dependency needs when they were young. This makes them very angry and hostile, and they begin to test the love of those to whom they are close, to see if those to whom they are close will reject them if they make enough demands. All of the time they are anticipating rejection. Eventually, they are rejected because they have set themselves up in such a way as to get rejected. This leads to even more fear of getting close to others. Thus, they do not get close. Moreover, as a result of not getting close, their dependency needs become even greater and their anger in-

creases, and on the cycle goes. There are individuals who so fear rejection that they will reject someone they are close to because subconsciously they fear if they do not reject him, they will end up getting rejected by him.

13. *Deal with fear of rejection by changing behavior*. Individuals who are depressed and going through the cycle mentioned above, adding to their depression, can change this pattern by changing their own behavior. They must learn that they can get close to other people. They must learn that individuals will not always disappoint them. They must learn to be more realistic in the demands they make on others instead of testing the love of others. They must learn to go ahead and take the chance of getting close. They must learn to stop rejecting others. They must be wary of the defense technique of projection. In short, they must break the rejection cycle by changing their behavior patterns.

14. *Recognize the anger*. Depressed individuals are often very angry individuals, and yet many of them do not realize this. It is not uncommon for a patient to say that he is not angry, even though his fist is clenched and his face stern. As depressed individuals are able to recognize and admit their anger and gain insight into it, they begin to get better. Thus recognition of the anger is not enough. They must go ahead and also deal with the anger. Ways to deal with this anger have been discussed thoroughly in chapter 13.

15. *Be careful with introspection*. While insight can be of great assistance in helping people overcome their depression, it can become very dangerous if it goes beyond healthy insight into introspection. This is a special danger for depressed individuals because they tend to be overly introspective anyway. We encourage our patients to limit their time of introspection to therapy sessions, or perhaps to periods when they are talking with a close friend. We encourage them not to spend hours of introspection trying to figure everything out, because they tend to be overly critical and overly hard on themselves. If the individuals are so caught up within themselves that they cannot

stop being introspective, we encourage them at least to set aside a certain portion of their day for thinking about their problem, and to refuse to think about it all day long. If they think about it all day long every day, they will use up all their emotional reserves, and their depression will become worse. One reason that introspection is not good for depressed individuals is that much of their introspection is not objective. They are overly pessimistic and negative in their thinking, and their evaluation of themselves and their situation is often not realistic. When depressed individuals find themselves becoming introspective, they need to get busy doing something and to do all within their power to stop this introspection.

16. *Stop playing God*. As stated previously, in cases of depression the individual has turned against himself. He has turned his anger on himself. He feels he deserves to be punished. When he feels miserable and depressed, he is getting just what he deserves. In a sense, he is playing God. He needs to ask God to forgive him of his sins in the past and to let God decide on the proper discipline. It may be that God will not choose any further discipline at all. And, if that is God's wish, then the depressed individual needs to learn to abide by God's will and stop punishing himself.

17. *Stop getting even*. Many depressed individuals use their depression to manipulate others and to get even. Depression can be a powerful tool by which to make others suffer and by which to manipulate them. Depression is a way to relieve pent-up anger. Thus, some depressed individuals use their depression to relieve themselves of anger and get even with others. Depressed individuals may also use their depression as a way to gain attention from others. Depressed individuals need to learn healthy ways to gain the attention they so desire, and they need to find better ways to relieve their guilt. There are many productive, healthy things that they can do that will gain them this attention, attention which they may not even realize they need.

18. *Accept responsibility for the depression*. Many depressed individuals can begin to get over their depression if they accept

responsibility for their depression. By putting themselves in charge of their own lives they can begin to get better. In Philippians 4:13 the apostle Paul says, "I can do all things through Christ who strengthens me." This is similar to an old proverb which states, "Pray to God, but keep rowing to shore." When individuals say, "I just can't get over this depression," what they really mean is that they *won't* get over the depression. There is often some subconscious reason why they do not want to get over their depression. They may be gaining attention from it, or they may be manipulating others with it, or using it to punish themselves or someone else. They may even use it as an excuse for not getting out and doing something more productive.

19. *Choose healthy ways to cope*. Many individuals reinforce their depression by continuing to cope with the stresses in their life through unhealthy means. For example, they may continue to internalize anger. Also, they may continue their pattern for worrying, and thus use up all their mental energy. They may continue their pattern of being depressed simply because they are used to it, and it is at least a familiar way to cope. They can begin to get over their depression by finding new and healthy ways to cope. As mentioned above, exercise is an excellent way to take hostile energy and divert it into a more productive and healthy direction.

We need to be sure that we have some kind of social contact every day. In Philippians 2:4 the apostle Paul says, "Look not every man on his own things, but every man also on the things of others." It is healthy to get our minds off ourselves and onto others. In fact, this helps us to see our own problems more objectively. In the original Greek, this verse actually means that an individual should look *not only* on his own things *but also* on the things of others. We do need to look at our own problems and the issues that we face, but we should not become overly absorbed in those problems. Instead, we should also focus on helping others and, in turn, that helps us in dealing with our own problems.

A major way to ward off or to help overcome depression is to maintain a quiet time with the Lord every day. This helps us to ventilate to our Heavenly Father. It helps us to be close to someone who loves us with a supernatural and intimate love. It gives us confidence. It gives us hope. It helps us to see things more objectively. It gives us supernatural help through the very Word of God itself.

20. *Realize there is hope.* One way to achieve a good success rate in treating depression is to help people realize there is hope. Any individual can overcome depression; often the first step is for him to simply realize that there is hope. Recently, a Christian man told us that he had been depressed for twenty years and had seen at least a half dozen therapists during that time. When we told him there definitely was hope for him and that he could get over his depression, he exclaimed, "That's the first time anyone ever told me I could get well!" Within a month he felt better than he had for twenty years. There definitely is hope.

21. *Avoid the sin trap.* One reason some individuals suffer from depression is that they are involved in sin. One study among adolescents revealed that 80 percent of males and 72 percent of females feel that premarital intercourse is acceptable, even though it can result in much grief.[5] Much depression and grief can be avoided by refusing to engage in sinful behavior. For example, one of the greatest regrets among women is having chosen to have an abortion. Having had premarital and extramarital affairs also grieves them a great deal.

Furthermore, not only does sin result in depression, but when people get depressed, they often react by engaging in even more sinful behavior in an attempt to relieve the emotional pain they feel. But the result is that they feel even more depressed. We would do well to heed the words of King Solomon in regards to sinful behavior: "Avoid it, pass not by it, turn from it, and pass away" (Proverbs 4:15).

22. *Avoid the guilt trap.* Depressed individuals feel a great amount of guilt. They will benefit by learning to deal with their guilt. If the guilt is true guilt, then it is simply a matter of either confessing it to God (I John 1:9), or perhaps dealing with that guilt in relationship to another person (Acts 24:16). God desires

that we confess our sins and then forget about them and move on. If the guilt is false guilt, as is often the case in depression, the individual needs to educate himself concerning the grace and mercy of God. As stated earlier, many obsessive-compulsive individuals feel intense false guilt. Merely by gaining insight into their personality much of this guilt can be relieved. Memorizing verses such as Lamentations 3:21-23 can also be of much help.

23. *Manipulate the environment.* Individuals can recover from depression by either learning to cope with stress from within or by relieving the stress through environmental manipulation. While we spend much time helping individuals learn new means of coping, we also encourage them to do whatever they can to alter and relieve external stresses. Perhaps their depression is partially brought on by working too hard, and they can alter the amount of external stress they are experiencing by working fewer hours. Perhaps their depression is caused by a sin they are committing, and they can relieve the external stress by stopping the sinful behavior. There are often many things individuals can do to manipulate the amount of external stress they are experiencing, and thus significantly help to relieve their depression.

24. *Respond–don't react.* Many depressed individuals react very strongly when stressful situations come up. They may become overly aggressive and attack another individual. They feel bad about this afterward. As they learn to control their reactions and to respond rather than to react, they begin to feel better about themselves and the way they are handling the situation.

25. *Increase self-esteem.* Individuals who are depressed usually have an extremely low level of self-esteem. They will benefit by increasing their self-esteem. Christ told us to love our neighbor as we love ourselves; this implies that we should have a healthy self-image. We are able to give to others only as we have a healthy opinion of ourselves. If we develop a low opinion of ourselves, we become overly absorbed in ourselves and do not

have anything left to give to others.

Many Christians confuse the sin of pride with the godly attribute of loving ourselves in a healthy way. However, these two (pride and self-worth) are really opposites. Actually, the more inferior a person feels the more he will compensate with false pride, and develop a "better than thou" attitude toward others. This is to cover up his own feelings of inadequacy.

How can we raise our self-image to an appropriate level? There are basically three ways. The first is to grow in our relationship to Christ. The second is to grow in our relationships with other individuals. The third is to set realistic goals and work toward those goals.

First, as we grow in our relationship with Christ, we will develop a better self-image. We will be doing what we know is important. We will be helping to transform our minds from within through the Spirit of Christ. Nothing can be more healthy than this. Nothing can help to make for a sounder self-image. We will not only be gaining insight into ourselves, but we will have a resource to help change ourselves as we need to.[6] Growing in Christ is the most important way to work on our self-image.

The second major way to improve our self-image is to improve our relationship to other individuals. Although it is unhealthy to depend too much upon others for our own self-image, a certain amount of this is present in all of us, and is healthy. Most of us to a certain degree evaluate how we are doing by noting how we relate to others and the feedback we get from others. As we are able to develop more intimate relationships with others, our self-image improves. All of us need love from at least one other individual. This is basic and of utmost importance to our self-image. In fact, a lack of such love is one of the central core issues in many emotional problems.

A third major way to improve our self-image is through setting realistic goals and obtaining those goals. Through setting realistic goals and accomplishing them we can say to ourselves that we are important and have a feeling of worth.

26. *Approach the depression on a spiritual, psychological, or physical level*. Another way to deal with depression is to approach it on

a spiritual, psychological, or physical level depending upon which is involved. Each of these levels breaks down into certain categories; by understanding the specific problems and specific categories, one will be able to deal with his problem. Following is an outline of treatment measures for spiritual, psychological, and physical problems as presented in the book, *Christian Psychiatry.*[7] This chart outlines, step by step, how to deal with four causes of spiritual depression and several causes of psychological or physical depression.

I. Spiritual problems (see I Thessalonians 5:14).
   A. A need to know Christ (see Romans 1:16).
      1. During the course of counseling (after a relationship has been built) ask the counselee about his religious background.
      2. Share the gospel.
      3. Write out verses on salvation (see John 1:12; Romans 3:23; 6:23).
      4. Keep it simple.
      5. Give the counselee an opportunity to believe in Christ.

   B. A need to grow in Christ (see I Peter 2:2).
      1. Engage the counselee in a Bible study series on discipleship. The Bible study should focus on the basics in the Christian life (God's Word, prayer, Christian fellowship, and witnessing). Help the counselee form a solid foundation in each of these areas and thus a balanced (healthy, mature) Christian life.
      2. Have the counselee memorize three verses per week.
      3. Help the counselee figure out a specific plan for having a quiet time.
      4. Help the counselee become involved in a church. For further support help the counselee become involved with a smaller group within the church (a minichurch).

   C. A need to deal with a specific sin (see II Thessalonians 3:5).

1. Listen to the counselee and build a relationship.
2. Confront the counselee about his sin.
3. Ask for a one-week commitment (until the next appointment) to avoid the sin.
4. Have the counselee complete a short Bible study (approximately one page) on the problem area prior to the next appointment. Make the focus of the Bible study on personal application.
5. Ask the counselee to memorize three verses per week that deal with the problem.
6. For support and strength to overcome the temptation, help the counselee to become involved with fellow Christians in a church, mini-church, or another Christian group.
7. Ask the counselee to have a quiet time daily.

D. Demonic influences (demon possession or demon oppression).

1. Share the concepts in Ephesians 6.
2. Point out that Satan is aware of the particular temptations one is prone to and the weaknesses he has.

II. Psychological problems.

A. Psychophysiologic problems (ulcer, colitis, high blood pressure, etc.).

1. Advise the counselee concerning the spiritual and psychological aspects of his problem.
2. Refer to the local medical doctor for treatment of the physical aspect of the problem.
3. If needed, work with another professional concerning the psychological aspect.

B. Personality trait or personality disorder.

1. Discern the personality traits and vary your counseling approach accordingly. For example, do not approach an individual with hysterical traits in the same manner as you would approach an individual suffering from depression.
2. *Listen* with empathy as the counselee tells of his problem, past history, and feelings.

3. Explain to the counselee the strengths and potential weaknesses of his personality. Help him gain *insight*.
4. Help the counselee to formulate a specific *plan of action* to deal with his problem.
5. If needed, work with another professional who has training in psychology or psychiatry.

C. Neurosis (a biologic and social impairment).
1. Discern the type of neurosis and approach accordingly.
2. *Listen* with empathy as the counselee tells of his problem, past history, and feelings.
3. Explain to the counselee what he is doing and what is happening to him. Help him gain *insight*.
4. Help the counselee formulate a specific *plan of action* to deal with his problem.
5. If needed, work with another professional who has training in psychology or psychiatry. This may be needed when a threat of suicide or homicide exists. It will also be necessary if the counselor realizes the problem is beyond his capability. If medication is needed, refer to a psychiatrist. If psychological tests are needed, refer to a psychologist. Of course, either can give the counselee therapy.

D. Psychosis (a loss of contact with reality).
1. Work with another professional (local medical doctor, psychiatrist, or psychologist).
2. Since the brain chemistry is usually altered in psychosis, medication is needed. Thus, referral should be made to a psychiatrist.

III. Physical problems. Of course, physical problems will need to be referred to the local medical doctor or psychiatrist; but since spiritual and psychological factors may also be present, the counselor may wish to work with the doctor. The minister or layman should be especially alerted to the following physical problems that are often confused with psychological or spiritual problems.

A. Hyperkinesis (hyperactive child).
B. High or low blood-sugar levels.
C. Thyroid problems.
D. Organic brain syndrome of old age.
E. Biochemical depression.

27. *Learn to laugh*. As individuals learn to bring more humor into their lives and to laugh more they can really improve. Laughter relaxes us as almost nothing else can. Many individuals improve as soon as they learn no one is perfect (not even they) and as they begin to laugh at their own perfectionistic demands or other shortcomings.

Probably no topic is approached so naively, defensively, or simplistically as human depression. What is depression? What causes depression? How can I avoid it? How can I get over it if I am already suffering its pain? Is happiness really a choice, or am I a victim of circumstances? If I choose to be happy, what path must I take to obtain happiness?

These are the questions which this book answers, and the answers are many and varied. There are no simple answers. There is no single cause for all depressions, even though pent-up anger is the root cause of the vast majority of depressions. There is no single solution, even though faith in Jesus Christ and in the principles of God's Word is at the root of all the solutions (known and unknown). The solutions may sometimes be very complex, but they do exist! Perhaps the future may bring some new, more rapid solutions. But even now, by applying the contents of this book, depression is 100 percent treatable. In fact, depression (over a period of weeks or months) is 100 percent curable. Indeed, *happiness is a choice!—your choice!*

APPENDICES AND NOTES

Appendix 1
Classifications of Depression

A brief review is in order before we can distinguish neurotic from psychotic depression.

1. *Sad affect*. The individual that is depressed looks depressed. Even when he tries to hide his feelings, he still looks depressed. His forehead is usually furrowed and the edge of his mouth is turned downward. He either cries often or wants to cry often. As women become depressed they often stop putting on make-up, and as men become depressed they often stop shaving. Thus, a sad facial expression is one of the major symptoms of depressive neurosis.

2. *Painful thinking*. As individuals become more and more depressed, they have what is known as painful thinking. It actually is painful to think. It is painful to think for they feel blue, sad, hopeless, helpless, worthless, and guilty. They ruminate much over past mistakes, and guilt permeates their thinking. They feel so unhappy they can hardly stand it. They are pessimistic, and their future looks dark. They regard themselves

complete failures as persons. They no longer get satisfaction out of life. Things they used to enjoy, they no longer enjoy. They often feel they are being punished. They have a dislike of themselves and they feel disappointed and disgusted with themselves. They accuse themselves; they are very critical of themselves and blame themselves for many things. Their painful thinking may go to the point that they wish themselves harm. They may have thoughts of suicide. They become irritable and are hard to get along with. As they become more and more depressed, they begin to withdraw socially. They lose interest in the people and activities that used to interest them. They have a hard time making up their mind and are indecisive on even small matters. Their self-image is very low and they do not like themselves. They begin to develop difficulty in performing. They have a hard time doing their job, and the depression may develop to the point they may not be able to do their job at all. They have difficulty deriving pleasure from their achievements. They have painful thinking.

3. *Psychomotor retardation*. As individuals become more and more depressed, they develop additional physical symptoms. They often appear as though they are in slow motion. They may move slowly and talk slowly. Often they experience difficulty in their sleep. Maybe they are sleeping too much, or they sleep too little. They either have difficulty going to sleep or, more commonly, they wake up too early in the morning as the depression becomes more severe. They either eat too much or eat too little. They may initially eat too much in order to try to escape, but later their appetite disappears and they lose weight. In fact, probably nothing will cause a person to lose so much weight as depression except perhaps cancer. Their mental and physical responses are slow; hence the name *psychomotor retardation*. It may take twice the time to perform a task that they have performed in the past. There is often a change in the sex drive (usually a decrease). They may suffer from diarrhea or more often from constipation. They have somatic complaints that may range from headaches to stomach-aches. They feel a constant fatigue and they are hardly able to get going in the morning. In fact, the morning is the worst part of the day. They become more worried than usual about their physical health.

4. *Overanxiety*. Anxiety often accompanies depression. As individuals become more and more depressed they become more and more anxious. They are more irritable than usual and get more upset than usual. They are less able to cope than they could in the past.

5. *Distorted thinking*. As individuals become more and more depressed, they gradually move from neurotic depression to psychotic depression and their thinking actually becomes distorted. They may hear critical condemning voices. Recently a patient of ours heard very accusing voices. But as the depression began to lift, the voices began to go away. Individuals with distorted thinking may experience either hallucinations (for example, they may hear voices) or delusions. Because of their loss of esteem they may develop delusions of grandeur. They may imagine that they are Napoleon or that the Mafia is after them.

When individuals have the first three symptoms listed above (sad affect, painful thinking, and psychomotor retardation), they have a *neurotic depression*.[1] If anxiety is also present and is very prominent, they have what is known as an *agitated depression* (this is still classified as neurotic depression).[2] The depression becomes a *psychotic depression* when the fifth symptom (distorted thinking) is added.[3]

The official way to classify depression is by the DSM II Model, that is, the *Diagnostic and Statistical Manual of Mental Disorders*.[4] The DSM II Manual is considered the "bible of psychiatry." It is the official classification system in psychiatry. It is currently being reorganized into a DSM III Model, but at the present there are ten classifications that pertain to a depressive disorder. They are (1) involutional melancholia; (2) manic-depressive illness, manic type; (3) manic-depressive illness, depressive type; (4) manic-depressive illness, circular type; (5) psychotic depressive reaction; (6) schizophrenia, schizoaffective type, excited; (7) schizophrenia, schizoaffective type, depressed; (8) depressive neurosis; (9) cyclothymic personality; and (10) adjustment reaction of adult life with depressive features. It will be helpful to give a brief description of each of these disorders.

1. *Involutional melancholia*. The diagnosis of involutional melancholia is reserved for depressions that begin in middle life.

There is apparently no precipitating cause. The individual has never suffered from a depression before, but this depression is very severe (perhaps even to a psychotic degree).

2. *Manic-depressive illness, manic type*. Manic-depressive illness, manic type, is characterized by a feeling of euphoria, by rapid speech, and by increased motor activity. The person may fly from one topic to another and may also be characterized by poor judgment. For example, individuals in a manic state have gone out and bought several cars in the same day or made very poor financial judgments. Though the person feels extremely good, this feeling of euphoria is often just a cover-up for the underlying depression. This manic-depressive illness actually goes to the point of psychosis. For example, in her manic phase of depressive psychosis one lady thought she was the Virgin Mary. Individuals in this state are often very uninhibited and sexual matters will often be of great importance to them. They will often parade around the psychiatric ward almost nude. Religion may be another topic that will become important to them; they may talk in a religious jargon. Probably more than any other depressive disorder, manic-depressive illness carries a hereditary predisposition. It does run in families. Current research seems to show that it may be carried by the X-chromosome. Cyclothymic personality traits (see below, number 9) carried to an extreme would be manic-depressive psychosis.

3. *Manic-depressive illness, depressive type*. Manic-depressive illness, depressive type, is characterized by traits opposite to those of the manic type. For example, the individual will feel low, blue, and sad in his mood. He will move very slowly and will often talk slowly. He may have had previous manic episodes, and now he has swung into the depressive cycle. An individual who has true manic-depressive illness, depressive type, can be indistinguishable from an individual with unipolar or regular depressive reactions. The genetic history may indicate which type of depression is present. Individuals with the depressive type of manic-depressive illness respond to regular medication and treatment for depression whereas the manic-

type individuals discussed above respond to a kind of medication known as lithium.

4. *Manic-depressive illness, circular type*. Manic-depressive illness, circular type, is characterized by alternating between manic episodes and depressive episodes. For example, the individual may be manic for several weeks; this may be followed by a period of regular and normal activities. Then the individual may experience periods of depression. It seems that during the depression phase the individual is overcome by self-criticism from within. He becomes one of his own worst enemies as he attacks himself. In the manic phase, on the other hand, he seems to have overcome his enemy from within; he becomes very elated and feels euphoric at having overcome the self-critical nature from within. He then becomes normal in activity as he is able to strike a balance between the two. But then again the self-criticism from within may win over and he becomes depressed, and so the cycle goes.

5. *Psychotic depressive reaction*. The psychotic depressive reaction is characterized by the usual symptoms of depression mentioned above. That is, the individual has a sad affect and painful thinking—he feels blue, sad, hopeless, helpless, and guilty. He has biological symptoms and anxiety. In addition to this, he develops delusions or distorted thinking. He may have auditory hallucinations and hear critical voices. He may imagine that the Mafia is after him. This type of thinking differs from painful thinking only in degree. The patient moves from painful thinking into completely distorted and delusional thinking. This is a psychotic depressive reaction.

6. *Schizophrenia, schizoaffective type, excited*. This is a type of schizophrenia that is also characterized by a mood disorder. Perhaps a distinction should be made at this point between schizophrenia and manic-depressive psychosis. Schizophrenia is a disease that is characterized mainly by a thought disorder and perhaps secondarily by a mood disorder, such as is seen in schizoaffective schizophrenia. Manic-depressive illness, on the

other hand, is characterized mainly by a mood disorder and perhaps secondarily by a thought disorder. In other words, in schizophrenia, the thought disorder is the primary problem—the individual cannot keep his thoughts together. It is as though someone took his brain and shattered it on concrete. He is bombarded by many thoughts and often cannot give coherent verbal expression to them. He may very well have what is known as loose associations as he goes from one topic to another with no seeming connection between them.

Thus, the schizoaffective schizophrenic is characterized first of all by a thought disorder. He has the usual symptoms of schizophrenia. He has a flat (nonexpressive) affect or facial expression. He has loose associations. He is very ambivalent and cannot make up his mind. He is very autistic and turned inward. Thus, he has the usual four A's of schizophrenia—flat *a*ffect, loose *a*ssociations, *a*mbivalence, and *a*utism. He may have the secondary symptoms of schizophrenia such as auditory or visual hallucinations and delusions. His thoughts are fragmented. He has poor judgment and is often very regressed and withdrawn socially. In addition to these schizophrenic symptoms, the schizoaffective also has a mood problem. If he is the excited type of schizoaffective schizophrenic, he is very high and euphoric in his mood.

7. *Schizophrenia, schizoaffective type, depressed*. This disorder is the same as the one just described, except that the mood disorder secondary to the thought disorder is depression instead of excitation.

8. *Depressive neurosis*. A depressive neurosis is characterized first of all by the individual's being neurotic rather than psychotic. The individual is incapacitated both biologically and socially for an extended period of time. If he is incapacitated biologically he has biological symptoms; for example, he cannot eat or sleep, or he loses weight, or he gains weight, or he cannot perform sexually. These are biological symptoms. He also has social symptoms. For example, he will not do his work. Because of these social symptoms others notice that something is wrong. An individual is neurotic when he is incapacitated biologically

and socially for an extended period of time (several months). A depressive neurosis is characterized by a sad affect, painful thinking, biological symptoms, and overt anxiety. Although this individual is very miserable and feels very depressed, he is in contact with reality. He does know who he is, where he is, and what is going on around him, whereas the psychotic individual has lost contact with reality.

9. *Cyclothymic personality*. A cyclothymic personality disorder is characterized by the individual's having certain lifelong personality patterns. He also has certain predictable defense mechanisms. His personality pattern usually begins at a very early age and remains with him throughout life. A cyclothymic personality disorder is similar to manic-depressive psychosis but it is not as severe. Throughout life the individual is high and elated for a period of time, then quite depressed for a period of time. Or he may remain quite elated throughout life or quite depressed throughout life. In other words, he can be high, low, or alternate between the two throughout his life. Following is a list of cyclothymic personality traits: Some of these border on the manic phase of manic-depressive psychosis.

1. Recurring and alternating periods of depression and elation (mood swings).
2. Periods of elation.
3. Ambition.
4. Warmth.
5. Enthusiasm.
6. Optimism.
7. High energy.
8. Increased speech (talkativeness).
9. Increased motor activity (overactive physically and mentally).
10. Flight of ideas (racing from one topic to another).
11. Poor judgment.
12. Irritability.

13. Accelerated speech.
14. Extroversion.
15. Likability.
16. Contagious humor.
17. Quick anger.
18. Success in whatever endeavors one undertakes.
19. Insensitivity.
20. Similarity to the manic phase of manic-depressive illness.
21. Impulsiveness.
22. Interference with vocational and domestic adjustments.
23. Making commitments which cannot be fulfilled.
24. Starting things which cannot be finished.
25. Good spirits.
26. Effervescence.
27. Behavior which can be trying to one's family in the early morning.
28. Habitual cheerfulness.
29. Euphoria.
30. Inability to keep one's mind on a continuous train of thought.
31. Defenses against depression.
32. Denial.
33. Reversal of affect.
34. Hostile humor.
35. Embarrassing comments.
36. Little compassion.
37. Defensive projection.
38. Conquering superego.
39. Supreme self-confidence.
40. Acquiring possessions normally out of one's financial range.

41. Frantic drive.
42. Flight from punishment.
43. Family history of relatives similarly affected.
44. Excess gaiety.
45. Lack of inhibition.
46. Ecstasy.
47. Nudity.
48. Religious jargon.
49. Unrestrained good humor until frustrated—at this point the humor becomes caustic.
50. Insulting speech, sarcasm.
51. Grandiosity.
52. Lack of logic.
53. Allusions to one's outstanding personal achievements.
54. Easy distractability.
55. Absence of self-criticism.
56. Little true self-awareness.
57. Tendency to blame others.
58. Extravagant enterprises.
59. Exhibitionism.
60. Seductive behavior.
61. Hoarseness as a result of increase in speech.
62. Creation of interpersonal havoc with one's family.
63. Exploitation of the vulnerability of others.
64. Projection of responsibility.
65. Progressive testing of limits.
66. Maneuvering others to one's advantage.
67. Difficulty falling asleep.
68. Desire to be the central figure in the group.

69. Buoyancy.

70. Refusal to acknowledge one's illness.

71. Purposeless activity.

10. *Adjustment reaction of adult life with depressive features.* This diagnosis is reserved for temporary disorders of any severity that occur in persons with no apparent pre-existing mental disorders who are responding to an overwhelming environmental stress. The symptoms include some depressive features, and are readily resolved as the individual undergoes brief psychotherapy and as the stressful situation diminishes. For example, grief reaction may be diagnosed as an adjustment reaction.

Appendix 2
Case Studies of Depressed Individuals

Following are case histories which illustrate some of the early environmental factors involved in the development of depression. Specific details are changed.

Case 1. A young female was very depressed. She described *her mother as a very strict disciplinarian and very moody*. Whenever the patient would do something wrong, her mother would use the silent treatment for discipline. The patient stated that her *mother was a worrier. Not only did her mother suffer from periodic depression, but her grandmother did also*. The patient had a better relationship with her father than with her mother, but *she "could not" communicate with her father either*. The patient stated that *both of her parents were pessimistic*.

Case 2. A middle-aged female experienced depression and explosive episodes. The patient's history revealed that she had had a very difficult early environment. *During her first twelve years of life, she was in poor health and suffered from feelings of inadequacy. She had a low self-concept*. She also stated that she was not close to her mother, and that *she felt her mother accepted her on a performance basis*. She resented the fact that her mother first began to really accept her when she became good in sports during her teen-age years. The patient said that her mother loved her when she did what her mother wanted her to do, but that if she did not do what her mother wanted her to do, there was "suppressed rejection."

Case 3. A young female presented a case of depression. She said that her *mother was hostile and outspoken*. The mother would slap the daughter when they had arguments. The patient said that her mother was loving whenever she did what her mother wanted her to do, but otherwise her mother was cold and hostile. The patient said that her mother would make her feel guilty about various things. *The mother would lower the daughter's self-image by various statements about the daughter's personal appearance*. The patient stated that her mother was harsh in discipline.

Case 4. A thirty-year-old male complained of depression. This patient stated that although *his mother was overprotective in some ways, he still did not feel accepted by her*. In fact, the patient stated that his mother gave him to an aunt, who took care of him most of the time.

Case 5. A middle-aged female complained of marital conflict. She was also very depressed. Her depression centered on her marital conflict. However, some factors in her early environment contributed to the problem. *She never really knew her father since he had been very dedicated to his business*. Though her father was strict, her mother was even more so. The patient stated that *her mother was "totally strict and totally legalistic."* The patient stated that she was not allowed to make any decisions for herself. She said that her mother destroyed any natural relations. For example, the mother researched the past of any boy her daughter dated; if any minor fault was found, further dates with that boy were forbidden.

Case 6. A sixty-year-old female complained of depression. One of her chief worries was that she feared that she might not be a Christian. She feared this although she had been very active in church for years and years. Her history revealed that *her mother had never accepted her. The patient's mother had never loved nor kissed her. As a result, years later she thought that the Lord could not accept her*. During the course of therapy the patient did improve. She said that she was especially helped by a Bible study on the concept of grace. She improved as she learned of the unmerited love of God.

Case 7. A middle-aged male complained of depression. This patient stated that his *biological father had been subject to depression. The biological father committed suicide* when the patient was five or six years of age. Not only was the patient's biological father depressed, but his stepmother was also. The patient described his *stepmother as "nervous and depressed."* The patient stated that his stepmother would in anger discipline him.

Case 8. A young male complained of depression. He gave a history of his father being passive and his mother domineering. He stated that his mother was "bossy." He also said that *his wife was domineering just as his mother had been.*

Case 9. A female in her middle thirties complained of depression. *She described her father as being sad and withdrawn and stated that her mother had been nervous and depressed.* She stated that her mother had suffered so severely from depression that she had, in fact, committed suicide.

Case 10. A female in her early forties complained of depression. *She described her mother as unloving, unconcerned, and indifferent.* During the patient's early life, she had lived on a ranch with her family. She stated that few people were around and that she was a loner.

Case 11. A fifty-year-old male complained of anxiety and depression. He stated that his mother never showed any affection and that *he felt rejected by his mother.* He said that his mother was very strict. For example, before the patient's first date, his mother had given his girl friend a lecture. The patient said that his mother was domineering and that his father was passive. He said his mother was also overprotective and that she had even dominated him after he married. The patient said that he felt inferior and had a low self-image when he was young. *He said he always wanted to win his mother's acceptance.*

The following story illustrates the cycle we have met in these case studies—unmet dependency needs, hostility, fear of rejection, and avoidance of closeness to others.

A depressive is driving down a country road and has a flat tire. He looks in his trunk for a jack. Not finding one, he spots a farmhouse about a quarter of a mile away. There is a truck in the front yard. He says to himself, "I'll go borrow his jack." As he approaches the house he is feeling bad because of (1) his failure to have a jack and (2) his having to depend on someone else for help. As he gets nearer the farmhouse he begins to expect rejection. He gets angry over his expectation of rejection. He becomes more and more angry at his unmet dependency needs and projects onto the farmer the anger he feels toward himself for needing the jack. By the time the farmer responds to the knock on the door, the depressive is so angry he yells, "Keep your jack." This guarantees that he does not get the jack and he walks back more convinced than ever that he cannot depend on people.[1]

Appendix 3
Drugs and the Treatment of Depression

Physical Effects of Stress

Internalized stresses result in adrenalin release. The adrenal gland is the "fight or flight" gland, and its hormones are always released under stress. Initially there is an increase in adrenalin (epinephrine) and noradrenalin (norepinephrine). However, as stress continues and anxiety is not dealt with, biochemical changes will begin to occur in the body. Eventually, depletion of noradrenalin (norepinephrine) occurs. We hypothesize that with stress the system will initially release more adrenal hormones, but if the stress continues, the system eventually becomes depleted, and the norepinephrine level becomes low. In view of the function of norepinephrine this is very important. Norepinephrine is a neurotransmitter in the limbic system of the brain which controls emotions such as depression or euphoria. Among other important neurotransmitters are serotonin and dopamine. These neurotransmitters also are responsible for dreaming, as was discussed earlier. When the norepinephrine decreases to a certain level, the depression becomes physical and biochemical (in addition to being emotional). At this point, a tricyclic antidepressant can be given which, within a matter of two to three weeks, will usually relieve many symptoms of the depression. As stated previously, norepinephrine is a neurotransmitter that transmits impulses across the synaptic clefts in the limbic system of the brain. After it carries the impulse across the synaptic cleft, it goes back, is taken up by the presynaptic neuron, is broken down, and metabolized. Tofranil, a tricyclic antidepressant, works by blocking the presynaptic neuron from taking up the norepinephrine. Thus the norepinephrine levels at the receptor site increase.

Various antidepressants work in somewhat different ways biochemically.[1] For example, amitriptyline (Elavil) is a weak inhibitor of norepinephrine uptake, but is a potent inhibitor of serotonin uptake. This may explain why one antidepressant may work better in one case, and another may work better for another person.

Tricyclic antidepressants may work by the deamination (breaking off of an amine group) of norepinephrine by mitochondrial monoamine oxidase. However, they are not monoamine oxidase inhibitors in the usual sense. They may also work by using intraneuronal membranes (mitochondrial membranes) to prevent norepinephrine from interacting with monoamine oxidase. In any event, the major way they work is by blocking the presynaptic neuron from taking up the norepinephrine. Thus there is an overall increase in norepinephrine. This accounts for the lifting of the depression.

It is important to note that the norepinephrine level is very important for other reasons. For example, it also affects the hypothalamus. The key regulator of the secretion of the hypothalamic-releasing factors is norepinephrine. Of course, the hypothalamic-releasing factors control the release of hormones from the pituitary or master gland. These hormones include growth hormones, luteinizing hormones, prolactin, thyroid-stimulating hormone, and adrenocorticotropic hormone. Thus, an endocrine disturbance can develop along with depression.

The hypothalamus also controls the autonomic nervous system, which sends nerve impulses to the various body organs. Thus, anxiety can cause the autonomic nervous system to produce a variety of physical symptoms to accompany the depression—a rapid heartbeat, an ulcer, a nervous stomach, and so forth.

The hypothalamus, which is affected by the level of norepinephrine in the brain, is also important as an influence on the immune system. The immune system is suppressed under stress. Thus, when an individual is anxious or depressed, he often has more colds and upper respiratory infections.

The Neurotransmitter Serotonin

One of the major trends in psychiatry in the last twenty years is research into biochemical factors involved in emotional problems.[2] This research has revealed that the two neurotransmitters in the brain that are depleted in depression are norepinephrine and serotonin. Some antidepressants act by increasing the norepinephrine (Norpramine). Others work by increasing the serotonin (Elavil) and some act by increasing both norepinephrine and serotonin (Tofranil, Aventyl).

A possible explanation as to how the norepinephrine becomes depleted as a result of stress has been given, but what about serotonin? A possible explanation is as follows:

Tricyclic Antidepressants

Prominent tricyclic antidepressants are Amitriptyline (Elavil, or Endep); Desipramine (Pertofrane, Norpramine); Doxepin (Sinequan, Adapin); Imipramine (Tofranil, S-K-Pramine); Nortriptyline (Aventyl); and Propriptyline (Vivactil). The exact daily dosage of these medications varies. A typical example would be 150 milligrams of Tofranil daily. Often the medication is given at bedtime because this allows its sedative effects to wear off before morning. In fact, the sedative effects are often helpful when the medication is given at bedtime. But even in this respect these drugs vary. For example, while Elavil acts as a sedative, Vivactil

THE PHYSICAL EFFECTS OF STRESS

Stressful Early Childhood Experiences

↓

Anxiety Created
(Anxiety I)

Anxiety Repressed into Subconscious

The brain functions as a computer with memory banks. Stressful memories are recorded and stored and can be replayed today in as vivid a form as when they initially occurred. They are aroused by current-day stress.

↓

Stressful Current-Day Experiences

↓

More Anxiety Created
(which we call Anxiety II)

↓

Anxiety II Arouses Anxiety I

We are anxious about our anxiety. We are also reacting to not only the current-day stresses, but also the repressed emotions of childhood. Anxiety from all three sources is repressed into the subconscious or unconscious.

Anxieties may be displaced onto an obsessive worry or phobia. Also, they may just be internalized, resulting in depression.

↓

Emotional Depression

As the anxieties from all three sources are internalized and left unresolved, the individual develops depression.

↓

Release of Adrenalin

This internal stress results in adrenalin being released (the adrenal gland is the "fight or flight" gland, and its hormones are always released under stress).

↓

Increased Adrenalin and Noradrenalin

Initially there is an increase in adrenalin and noradrenalin (also called norepinephrine).

↓

Stress Continues

If the anxieties are not dealt with, the internal stress will continue and biochemical changes will begin to occur.

↓

Depletion of Norepinephrine

The hypothesis is that with stress the system will initially release more adrenal hormones, but if the stress continues, the system eventually becomes depleted and the norepinephrine level low. In view of the function of norepinephrine, this is very important. Norepinephrine is a neurotransmitter in the limbic system of the brain which controls emotions such as depression or euphoria. Among other important neurotransmitters are serotonin and dopamine. When the norepinephrine decreases to a certain level, the depression becomes physical and biochemical (in addition to emotional).

Physical (Biochemical) Depression

Tricyclic antidepressant is given.

Hypothalamus Affected

The chief regulator of the secretion of the hypothalamic-releasing factors that affect the pituitary gland is norepinephrine.

Pituitary Gland Affected

Release of Hormones Affected

These include growth hormones, adrenocorticotropic hormone, luteinizing hormone, prolactin, and thyroid-stimulating hormone.

Possible Endocrine Disturbances

Suppressed Immune System

This results in more upper respiratory infections, colds, and viral infections.

Autonomic Nervous System Affected

The hypothalamus controls the autonomic nervous system with its nerves to the various body organs. Thus anxiety can cause the autonomic nervous system to produce a variety of physical symptoms to accompany the depression—a rapid heartbeat, an ulcer, a nervous stomach.

tends to act more as a stimulant. The effect of Tofranil runs a middle course between the two.

MAO Inhibitors

Another group of antidepressants is known as the monoamine oxidase inhibitors. Their effect is supposedly related to the inhibition of monoamine oxidase. Monoamine oxidase is responsible for the breakdown of norepinephrine. These drugs were initially used in the treatment of tuberculosis back in the 1950s. They were found to have a rather pronounced euphoric effect in some individuals, and thus were accidentally discovered to be antidepressants. These drugs include Nialamide (Niamid); Isocarboxazid (Marplan); Phenelzine (Nardil); Tranylcypromine (Parnate); and Pargyline (Eutonyl). These drugs have been used in the treatment of "atypical depression." In typical depression the depression in itself is only a part of the clinical picture. Other symptoms (features of hysteria, phobia, or anxiety) may also be prominent. These drugs are used less often today because they have been associated with troublesome side effects. One of the most dramatic side effects is paradoxical hypertension (elevated blood pressure). This can occur when someone using MAO inhibitors eats food that is high in tyramine content, such as cheese, chocolate, pickled herring, canned figs, yeast, game, red wines, chicken livers, broad pod beans, beer, meat extracts, and yogurt. Individuals on these drugs also have to be careful about certain medications such as amphetamines, adrenalin, noradrenalin, dopa, dopamine, certain cold remedies, nasal decongestants, and the novocaine used by dentists. Finally, it should be mentioned that the action of monoamine oxidase inhibitors may not be related merely to the inhibition of monoamine oxidase. In some cases, they may also work to block the uptake of norepinephrine in a manner similar to tricyclics.

Amphetamines

Amphetamines are another class of drugs that are used to deal with depression. Amphetamines may also work by effecting the level of norepinephrine in the brain. However, many individuals taking amphetamines alone to control their depression will have an additional depression after about two weeks from the onset of the medication. For this reason, they are not a good antidepressant medication. They are also addicting.

Stress

↓

Increase in cortisol

↓

Increase in tryptophan pyrrolase, a hepatic enzyme that results in the degradation of tryptophan, the precursor of serotonin

↓

Decrease in tryptophan

↓

Decrease in serotonin in the limbic part of the brain that controls mood

↓

Biochemical depression

↓

Thus, the depression started on an emotional level and ended up affecting the physical well-being as well.

Lithium

Another drug that has been tried in the treatment of depression is lithium. It has produced dramatic results. When lithium is started in the manic phase of manic-depressive psychosis, it seems to prevent the depressive phase from coming on and seems to help abate the manic phase. In other words, a person calms down, talks at a normal rate, and is no longer extremely euphoric; his mood is, as a matter of fact, rather normal. Also, he does not become depressed.

Naturally, the question arose as to whether lithium would be effective if used in the depressive phase of manic-depressive psychosis and whether it would be effective if used in regular unipolar depressions. Research is going on in this area, but the research tends to indicate that lithium is not as effective in the depressive phase as it is in the manic phase. The exact mechanism of how the lithium works is not known. Some feel that it works by influencing the electrolytes of the body—actually by influencing the sodium pump. Numerous other researchers turn to the possible effects of lithium on norepinephrine in the brain. Again, lithium does seem to have *some* influence on the levels of norepinephrine. However, the exact mechanisms for the beneficial effects of lithium remain uncertain at this time.

Major Tranquilizers

Another group of drugs that have been used in the treatment of certain cases of depression is the major tranquilizers. These drugs in general are not antidepressants. They will decrease anxiety and are usually used in cases of psychosis. Many of these drugs, in fact, precipitate a depression, or make a depression worse. However, a few of these drugs (for example, Mellaril) do seem to have some antidepressive qualities. We have personally noted that the major tranquilizer, Navanc, may have some antidepressive qualities.

Factors Affecting Dosage

Most psychiatric drugs are fat soluble and are concentrated in lipid tissues.[3] Therefore, women generally require more of a drug than men of the same weight range do, since women's body tissues contain a higher percentage of fat.

Another factor that can influence how much of a drug is needed is whether the individual is a smoker or not.[4] Individuals who smoke require more drugs.

Another factor that influences how much of a drug is needed is whether or not an individual is fasting.[5] Fasting is quite popular among some religious groups, but it can be very dangerous for individuals on psychiatric drugs. In individuals who are fasting the blood level increases excessively when psychiatric medicine is taken. So it is dangerous to take psychiatric medication and fast at the same time.

The concurrent use of other drugs can also alter the amount of antidepressant medication that is needed.[6] For example, barbiturates lower the blood level of the tricyclic antidepressants. Therefore more of an antidepressant drug is needed when the patient is also taking barbiturates. Other agents that lower the blood level of the tricyclic antidepressants (and therefore require an increase in the amount of tricyclic antidepressants to be taken by mouth) include expectorants that contain ammonia chloride and substances that lower the pH level, such as massive doses of vitamin C. Major tranquilizers can also affect the blood level of antidepressants that are being taken concurrently. Amphetamines such as Ritalin may add to the effects of tricyclics, since they decrease the speed of the elimination of these drugs from the body. Antacids will interfere with the absorption of tricyclic antidepressants, and, therefore, more medication will be required when they are being used concurrently. Elderly patients have some difficulty in absorbing the drugs, but, on the other hand, seem to benefit from lesser amounts. Tricyclic antidepressants can cause cardiac problems and are used with extreme caution in a patient with heart disease. Sometimes MAO inhibitors and tricyclic antidepressants are used concurrently, but this should be done with extreme caution. In most cases in which this is done, it is because of a resistant type of depression. Usually the tricyclic antidepressant is started first, and then an MAO inhibitor such as Parnate is added later.

Vitamin B_6, Thyroid Preparations, and Estrogen

General practitioners have long used vitamin B_6 to treat depression.[7] They have also long used certain thyroid preparations such as Cytomel to treat depression.[8] Research indicates that certain individuals do respond to Cytomel, to thyroid preparations, and to vitamin B_6. However, these are more the exception than they are the rule. Some cases of involutional, endogenous depressions will respond to a concomitant use of antidepressants with thyroid extract. Low-dose estrogen replacement is also often used for short periods of time along with antidepressants in involutional depression. The exact effect of estrogen on depression is uncertain. It is certain that estrogen does help the hot flashes and atrophic vaginitis.[9]

Megavitamins

It has recently been suggested that megavitamins are a panacea for almost every kind of emotional disorder. Individuals who propose the megavitamin theory have a large school of ardent followers. Because of the great interest in this field, intensive research has been undertaken by the medical society. Scientific research generally fails to confirm the notion that megavitamins are effective in the treatment of any emotional disorders.[10] Those individuals who turn to megavitamins are grasping for straws.

Medications That Cause Depression

Some medications will precipitate a depression. For example, some medication given for high blood pressure, such as reserpine, will do this. Also some birth control pills, at times, will precipitate a depression. Major tranquilizers can precipitate a depression. Minor tranquilizers such as valium can also precipitate a depression. Ritalin, which initially elevates the mood, can have a depressant effect two weeks later.

Alcohol, Tobacco, and Marijuana

Alcohol is a depressant, and yet millions of men and women use alcohol to drown their depressions. In 1950, there were three million alcoholics in America.[11] In 1977, there were over nine million.[12] Over one-half of the fifty thousand deaths annually on our highways are related to alcohol consumption.[13] The total cost for alcohol-related problems in 1950 was estimated at five billion dollars.[14] In 1977 it was twenty-four billion.[15] Alcoholism is a major problem. It is often caused by an underlying depression. In fact, one in every three alcoholics significantly benefits from antidepressant medication.

Adolescents begin to smoke *tobacco* for different reasons (peer pressure, sexual conflicts, and loneliness). The smoking does seem to provide a euphoric and tranquilizing effect. Individuals may become depressed after the cessation of smoking (a grief reaction to a loss).

However, it seems that the euphoric and tranquilizing effect is hardly worth the risk of cancer. Thirty-three million ex-smokers attest to this (since the Surgeon General's announcement regarding the hazards of cigarette smoking, thirty-three million Americans have stopped smoking).[16]

As Christians our body is the temple of the Holy Spirit. God desires that we take good care of it.

Some individuals who are depressed turn to *marijuana*. They enjoy the euphoric feeling and temporary lifting of the depression they get as a result of smoking the marijuana. Little do they know of the extremely dangerous consequences that can result from smoking marijuana.[17] Marijuana can cause permanent brain damage, lung damage, persistent personality changes, memory impairment, chromosome alterations, and motivational disturbances.

The scientific findings that marijuana is dangerous are convincing. Experiments with monkeys revealed there are immediate changes in behavior and brain wave activity. With time, the brain wave changes become permanent. Research has shown that individuals who have smoked at least two cigarettes of marijuana per day for two years have abnormal brain wave readings, and also have corresponding behavioral changes (such as chronic lethargy, loss of inhibition, etc.). Regular users of marijuana (once or twice per week) show evidence of memory impairment, sleep disturbance, swings of mood, and in general they function at a lower level.

Research also reveals that toxic substances in marijuana accumulate in the brain. These substances have long-range detrimental effects. They can permanently alter the fatty tissue of the brain. However, the changes are so slow and subtle that they may go unnoticed until after significant damage has been done. While marijuana does affect the pleasure centers in the brain, and thus can give a temporary euphoria, in the long run it produces a loss of motivation and even more depression.

The Menstrual Cycle and Depression

It is common for females to feel more anxious and depressed during their menstrual period. The question is: How much of this should be attributed to hormonal changes and how much to psychological and cultural factors? Hormonal changes certainly do occur and do make females more tense and more easily upset during their menstrual period. However, it seems that the degree of emotional upset that occurs is determined by psychological and cultural factors.

Shock Treatment

Shock treatment (or ECT) was introduced by Cerletti and Bani in 1938. It was used extensively until the 1950s in the treatment of emotional disorders, especially psychotic disorders.[18] In the early 1950s the phenothiazines and antidepressant drugs were introduced, so the use of ECT began to decrease. Personally we do not use ECT, but in certain cases it can give dramatic results. In general, there is a bad connotation associated with the use of ECT. Possibly this is because of the nature of the treatment itself—electroconvulsive therapy. Also, there may be a bad connotation because of reports of memory impairment associated with the use of ECT.

Today, ECT is used when the depression has been found to be resistant to the tricyclic medications. It is rarely the first line of treatment chosen. It is sometimes given to patients who have had adverse reactions to the tricyclic antidepressants. It is also sometimes used for severely suicidal patients. The reason for this is that the tricyclic antidepressants will not have an effect for a period of from two to three weeks, and the danger of suicide is thought to be pre-eminent. Today, usually five to eight treatments are given for depressive disorders. If the patients are not maintained following a course of ECT, between 30 and 40 percent of the cases will relapse within a year.[19] Of course, if they are maintained, this percentage will be significantly less. ECT has been proven to be relatively safe over the years. The death rate is probably between one in ten thousand and one in forty thousand treatments. Much has been made of the possible memory loss associated with ECT. Transient memory loss definitely does occur with the use of ECT. This may be anterograde or retrograde, and it increases with the number of treatments that are given. One must remember, when evaluating memory loss, that depression alone will also cause impairment in memory; therefore, the memory loss may not be due to the ECT. Actually, some patients have improved memory after ECT because the depression lifts.

It appears that the electric current that is passed through the brain during shock treatments discharges the norepinephrine in the brain. Actually, after a series of shock treatments has been given, there can be found in the urine a measurable increase of normetanephrine, the breakdown product of norepinephrine. Thus, ECT probably works by increasing the level of norepinephrine in the brain. Various other theories have been proposed.

In recent years the use of unilateral ECT has come into vogue. It has been known for some time that the two hemispheres of the brain function somewhat differently. This can be seen in cerebral infractions. For example, if the infraction occurs in the left hemisphere, depression seems to be more frequent; if the infraction occurs in the right hemisphere, euphoria and denial seem to be more frequent. On the basis of the theory that the two hemispheres function differently, the electrical current was passed through only one hemisphere—the nondominant hemisphere. It was found that this technique yielded less memory loss.

Major contraindications for ECT include serious cardiac disease and space-occupying intracranial lesions.

Insulin Coma Therapy

Brief mention should be made at this point of a type of therapy that is almost never used anymore—insulin coma therapy. This was used back in the 1940s.[20] A coma was brought on by the injection of insulin. Of course, the patient had to be monitored very closely.

Sleep Therapy

One other type of therapy that is rarely used today, but does deserve mention, is continuous sleep therapy. This was introduced in 1922 by a Swiss psychiatrist named Klesi.[21] He used drugs to induce long periods of sleep in psychiatric patients. The patients would go into a deep sleep for over a week at times, being awakened only for feeding and elimination of waste. The results in these cases seemed to be no better than those found with ECT.

These physical methods of treatment such as ECT, sleep therapy, and drugs are known collectively as somatic therapies.

Psychosurgery

Any attempt to influence the mind by surgery has been met with much resistance in the Christian community. Classical psychosurgery was introduced by Moniz in 1936.[22] Today it has been almost universally abandoned except for a highly specific type of psychosurgery which is used in cases such as temporal lobe epilepsy. Lesions in the temporal lobe can cause marked change in behavior. In marked contrast to the patient's normal behavior he may become irritable and aggressive. We do not recommend any type of psychosurgery, although the psychosurgery referred to above for a specific lesion is vastly different from the frontal lobotomies that were done in the 1930s and 1940s, which sometimes resulted in the complete loss of ambition or initiative.

Notes

Chapter 1
Who Gets Depressed?

1. *The Physician's Handbook on Depression* (Department of Psychiatry at the University of Pennsylvania, coordinated by Science and Medicine Publishing Company, 1977).
2. "Models of Affective Disorders," *Neuropsychopharmacology*, no. 6 in a series (1977).
3. W. G. Reese, "The Major Cause of Death," *Texas Medicine* 66 (Sept. 1970).
4. Philip Solomon and Vernon D. Patch, *Handbook of Psychiatry*, third edition (Lange Medical Publications, 1974), p. 336.
5. Shannon and Backus, "Depression," *Journal of the Arkansas Medical Society*, July, 1973.
6. Ibid.
7. Alfred M. Freedman et al., *Modern Synopsis of Psychiatry* (Baltimore: Williams and Wilkins, 1972), pp. 186-199, 264; Solomon and Patch, *Handbook of Psychiatry*, 57-58; Merrill T. Eaton, Jr., and Margaret H. Peterson, *Psychiatry* (New York: Medical Examination Publishing Co., 1969), 168, 199-209; Silvano Arieti et al., eds., *American Handbook of Psychiatry*, second edition (New York: Basic Books, 1974); Lawrence C. Kolb, *Modern Clinical Psychiatry* (Philadelphia: W. B. Saunders, 1973), pp. 110-114.

Chapter 2
What Are the Symptoms of Depression?

1. Shannon and Backus, "Depression," *Journal of the Arkansas Medical Society*, July, 1973.

Chapter 3
Is Suicide a Sin?

1. Merrill T. Eaton, Jr., and Margaret H. Peterson, *Psychiatry* (New York: Medical Examination Publishing Co., 1969); Philip Solomon and Vernon D. Patch, *Handbook of Psychiatry*, third edition (Lange Medical Publications, 1974), p. 333.

2. Ibid.

3. Ibid.

4. Ibid.

5. Ibid.

6. Ibid., p. 335.

7. Ibid., p. 336.

8. Ibid.

9. Gary R. Collins, *Overcoming Anxiety* (Santa Ana, CA: Vision House Publishers, 1973); Eaton and Peterson, *Psychiatry*.

10. Eaton and Peterson, *Psychiatry*; Jerome A. Motto, "Suicidal Patients in Clinical Practice," Weekly Psychiatry Update Series #18 (Biomedia, 1977); *Psychiatric Annals*, vol. 6, no. 11 (Nov. 1976—USV Pharmaceutical Mfg. Corp.); George Gilder, "In Defense of Monogamy," *Commentary*, November, 1974, pp. 31-36; "Evaluation of Suicidal Patients," *Psychiatric Digest*, September, 1974; "Suicide Notes and Risk of Future Suicide," *Psychiatric Digest*, October, 1974.

Chapter 5
Is Genetics a Good Excuse?

1. John M. Davis, *Depression: A Practical Approach* (New York: Medcom, 1974); "Models of Affective Disorders," *Neuropsychopharmacology*, no. 6 in a series (1977); Ronald L. Green, "Genetics of Affective Disorders," Weekly Psychiatry Update Series #35 (Biomedia, 1977); Alfred M. Freedman et al., *Modern Synopsis of Psychiatry* (Baltimore: Williams and Wilkins, 1972), p. 25; Philip Solomon and Vernon D. Patch, *Handbook of Psychiatry*, third edition (Lange Medical Publications, 1974), p. 192; "The Biochemical Basis of Psychopharmacology," excerpts from a discussion with Albert A. Kurland, Psychiatric Research Interview, Depression Notes #15.

Chapter 6
How Deep Do the Roots of Depression Run?

1. Shannon and Backus, "The Psychodynamics of Depression," *Journal of the*

Arkansas Medical Society, December, 1973; Philip Solomon and Vernon D. Patch, *Handbook of Psychiatry*, third edition (Lange Medical Publications, 1974), pp. 57-62; Alfred M. Freedman et al., *Modern Synopsis of Psychiatry* (Baltimore: Williams and Wilkins, 1972), p. 253; Otto Fenichel, *The Psychoanalytic Theory of Neurosis* (New York: W. W. Norton, 1945); L. Salzman, *The Obsessive Personality* (New York: Science House, 1968), pp. 107-127; Roger A. MacKinnon and Robert Michels, *The Psychiatric Interview in Clinical Practice* (Philadelphia: W. B. Saunders, 1971); Silvano Arieti et al., eds., *American Handbook of Psychiatry*, second edition (New York: Basic Books, 1974), pp. 57-62; Carl P. Malquist, "Childhood Depressions," Weekly Psychiatry Update Series #36 (Biomedia, 1977); Merrill T. Eaton, Jr., and Margaret H. Peterson, *Psychiatry* (New York: Medical Examination Publishing Co., 1969); Lawrence C. Kolb, *Modern Clinical Psychiatry* (Philadelphia: W. B. Saunders, 1973), pp. 535-538.

Chapter 8
Do "Nice Guys" Finish Last?

1. Otto Fenichel, *The Psychoanalytic Theory of Neurosis* (New York: W. W. Norton, 1945); L. Salzman, *The Obsessive Personality* (New York: Science House, 1968), pp. 3-14; Roger A. MacKinnon and Robert Michels, *The Psychiatric Interview in Clinical Practice* (Philadelphia: W. B. Saunders, 1971), pp. 89-97; Alfred M. Freedman et al., *Modern Synopsis of Psychiatry* (Baltimore: Williams and Wilkins, 1972), p. 208; Philip Solomon and Vernon D. Patch, *Handbook of Psychiatry*, third edition (Lange Medical Publications, 1974), p. 234; Merrill T. Eaton, Jr., and Margaret H. Peterson, *Psychiatry* (New York: Medical Examination Publishing Co., 1969), pp. 127-130; Lawrence C. Kolb, *Modern Clinical Psychiatry* (Philadelphia: W. B. Saunders, 1973), p. 91.

2. *Diagnostic and Statistical Manual of Mental Disorders*, second edition (Washington, DC: American Psychiatric Association, 1968).

3. Ibid.

4. Paul L. Adams, "Family Characteristics of Obsessive Children," *American Journal of Psychiatry* 128 (May 1972): 1414-17.

5. Paul Tournier, *A Doctor's Casebook in the Light of the Bible* (New York: Harper and Row, 1960).

6. O. Quentin Hyder, *The Christian's Handbook of Psychiatry* (Old Tappan, NJ: Fleming H. Revell, 1971).

Chapter 9
Can Depression Be Acted Out?

1. *Diagnostic and Statistical Manual of Mental Disorders*, second edition (Washington, DC: American Psychiatric Association, 1968); Roger A. MacKinnon and Robert Michels, *The Psychiatric Interview in Clinical Practice* (Philadelphia: W. B. Saunders, 1971), pp. 111-117; Alfred M. Freedman et al., *Modern Synopsis of Psychiatry* (Baltimore: Williams and Wilkins, 1972), p. 339; Philip Solomon and Vernon D. Patch, *Handbook of Psychiatry*, third edition (Lange Medical Publications, 1974), p. 218; Merrill T. Eaton, Jr., and Margaret H. Peterson, *Psychiatry* (New York: Medical Examination Publishing Co., 1969), p. 130;

Lawrence C. Kolb, *Modern Clinical Psychiatry* (Philadelphia: W. B. Saunders, 1973), pp. 91, 534.

Chapter 10
What Precipitating Stresses Bring on Depression?

1. Eugene S. Paykel, "Life Events and Emotional Disturbances," Weekly Psychiatry Update Series #9 (Biomedia, 1976).

2. Silvano Arieti et al., eds., *American Handbook of Psychiatry*, second edition (New York: Basic Books, 1974), pp. 294-298, 302-305; Merrill T. Eaton, Jr., and Margaret H. Peterson, *Psychiatry* (New York: Medical Examination Publishing Co., 1969), pp. 201, 361; Alfred M. Freedman et al., *Modern Synopsis of Psychiatry* (Baltimore: Williams and Wilkins, 1972), p. 495; Lawrence C. Kolb, *Modern Clinical Psychiatry* (Philadelphia: W. B. Saunders, 1973); Philip Solomon and Vernon D. Patch, *Handbook of Psychiatry*, third edition (Lange Medical Publications, 1974).

3. Arieti, *American Handbook of Psychiatry*, pp. 302-304.

4. *Diagnostic and Statistical Manual of Mental Disorders*, second edition (Washington, DC: American Psychiatric Association, 1968).

5. L. Salzman, *The Obsessive Personality* (New York: Science House, 1968), pp. 86-103.

Chapter 11
What Are the Personality Dynamics that Lead to Depression?

1. Marcus A. Krupp and Milton J. Chatton, *Current Diagnosis and Treatment* (Lange Medical Publications, 1973); "Models of Affective Disorders," *Neuropsychopharmacology*, no. 6 in a series (1977).

2. "Treatment with Psychotropic Drugs," Audio-Digest Foundation, *Psychiatry*, vol. 4, no. 19 (Oct. 13, 1975); "Management of Treatment-Resistant Depression," Audio-Digest Foundation, *Psychiatry*, vol. 5, no. 18 (Sept. 20, 1976); "Biological Dimensions in Psychiatry," Audio-Digest Foundation, *Psychiatry*, vol. 6, no. 1 (Jan. 10, 1977); Franklin W. Furlong et al., "Thyrotropin-Releasing Hormone: Differential Antidepressant and Endocrinological Effects," *American Journal of Psychiatry* 133 (Oct. 1976): 1187.

3. John M. Davis, *Depression: A Practical Approach* (New York: Medcom, 1974); "Models of Affective Disorders"; Steven Secunda, "Clinical Use of the Monamine Oxidase Inhibitors," Weekly Psychiatry Update Series #11 (Biomedia, 1976); Robert O. Friedel and Robert J. Bielski, "Prediction of Response to Antidepressant Medications," Weekly Psychiatry Update Series #12 (Biomedia, 1977); "Depression," *Psychiatric Annals*, vol. 3, no. 2 (Feb. 1973); *The Neuropharmacology of Depression* (Cincinnati: Merrell-National Laboratories, 1977); James W. Maas, "Biogenic Amines and Depression," *Archives of General Psychiatry*, vol. 32 (Nov. 1975); *Mandates Depression* (New York: Medcom, 1975); Ross J. Baldessarini, *The Basis for Amine Hypotheses in Affective Disorders: A Critical Evaluation* (American Medical Association, 1977); Frank Deleon-Jones

et al., *Diagnostic Subgroups of Affective Disorders and Their Urinary Excretion of Catecholamine Metabolites* (American Journal of Psychiatry Association, 1975).

4. "Models of Affective Disorders."

5. Ibid.

6. Shannon and Backus, "The Psychodynamics of Depression," *Journal of the Arkansas Medical Society*, December, 1973.

7. Ibid.

8. *The Physician's Handbook on Depression* (Department of Psychiatry at the University of Pennsylvania, coordinated by Science and Medicine Publishing Co., 1977).

9. Reprinted from *Comprehensive Textbook of Psychiatry*, eds. Harold Kaplan, Alfred Freedman, and Benjamin J. Saddock, second edition (Baltimore: Williams and Wilkins, 1975), p. 2400. Copyright 1967 by Pergamon Press, Inc. Used with permission.

10. Colin Murray Parkes, "Psychological Issues and Change," Weekly Psychiatry Update Series #33 (Biomedia, 1977).

11. Carl P. Malquist, "Depression in Children: Recognition," Weekly Psychiatry Update Series #24 (Biomedia, 1977); idem, "Childhood Depressions," Weekly Psychiatry Update Series #36 (Biomedia, 1977); James F. Masterson, "The Acting-Out Adolescent," Weekly Psychiatry Update Series #26 (Biomedia, 1977).

12. *The Physician's Handbook on Depression*; Aaron T. Beck, *Depression: Causes and Treatment* (Philadelphia: University of Pennsylvania Press, 1975); "Emotional Problems and Psychopharmacology," Audio-Digest Foundation, *Family Practice*, vol. 25, no. 29 (Aug. 1, 1977); "Drug Actions and Interactions," Audio-Digest Foundation, *Psychiatry*, vol. 6, no. 7 (April 11, 1977); Silvano Arieti et al., eds., *American Handbook of Psychiatry*, second edition (New York: Basic Books, 1974), p. 298; Merrill T. Eaton, Jr., and Margaret H. Peterson, *Psychiatry* (New York: Medical Examination Publishing Co., 1969), pp. 138, 303-313; Alfred M. Freedman et al., *Modern Synopsis of Psychiatry* (Baltimore: Williams and Wilkins, 1972), pp. 189, 197, 282-285; Lawrence C. Kolb, *Modern Clinical Psychiatry* (Philadelphia: W. B. Saunders, 1973), pp. 107-114, 357-387; Philip Solomon and Vernon D. Patch, *Handbook of Psychiatry*, third edition (Lange Medical Publications, 1974), pp. 57-62.

13. Frank B. Minirth, *Christian Psychiatry* (Old Tappan, NJ: Fleming H. Revell, 1977), pp. 130-143.

Chapter 12
Are There Some Basic Guidelines for a Happy Life?

1. W. Penfield, "Memory Mechanisms," *A.M.A. Archives of Neurology and Psychiatry* 67 (1952): 178-98.

Chapter 14
When Are Medication and Hospitalization Advantageous?

1. Merrill T. Eaton, Jr., and Margaret H. Peterson, *Psychiatry* (New York: Medical Examination Publishing Co., 1969), pp. 431-438; Alfred M. Freedman et al., *Modern Synopsis of Psychiatry* (Baltimore: Williams and Wilkins, 1972), pp. 27-29; Philip Solomon and Vernon D. Patch, *Handbook of Psychiatry*, third edition (Lange Medical Publications, 1974), pp. 451-461; *The Physician's Handbook on Depression* (Department of Psychiatry at the University of Pennsylvania, coordinated by Science and Medicine Publishing Co., 1977); *Psychiatric Annals*, vol. 6, no. 11 (Nov. 1976—USV Pharmaceutical Mfg. Corp.); Aaron T. Beck, *Depression: Causes and Treatment* (Philadelphia: University of Pennsylvania Press, 1975); "Treatment with Psychotropic Drugs," Audio-Digest Foundation, *Psychiatry*, vol. 4, no. 19 (Oct. 13, 1975); "Management of Treatment-Resistant Depression," Audio-Digest Foundation, *Psychiatry*, vol. 5, no. 18 (Sept. 20, 1976); "Biological Dimensions in Psychiatry," Audio-Digest Foundation, *Psychiatry*, vol. 6, no. 1 (Jan. 10, 1977); John M. Davis, *Depression: A Practical Approach* (New York: Medcom, 1974); "Models of Affective Disorders," *Neuropsychopharmacology*, no. 6 in a series (1977); Steven Secunda, "Clinical Use of the Monamine Oxidase Inhibitors," Weekly Psychiatry Update Series #11 (Biomedia, 1976); Robert O. Friedel and Robert J. Bielski, "Prediction of Response to Antidepressant Medications," Weekly Psychiatry Update Series #12 (Biomedia, 1977); "Depression," *Psychiatric Annals*, vol. 3, no. 2 (Feb. 1973); *The Neuropharmacology of Depression* (Cincinnati: Merrell-National Laboratories, 1977); James W. Maas, "Biogenic Amines and Depression," *Archives of General Psychiatry*, vol. 32 (Nov. 1975); *Mandates Depression* (New York: Medcom, 1975); Ross J. Baldessarini, *The Basis for Amine Hypotheses in Affective Disorders: A Critical Evaluation* (American Medical Association, 1977); Frank Deleon-Jones et al., *Diagnostic Subgroups of Affective Disorders and Their Urinary Excretion of Catecholamine Metabolites* (American Journal of Psychiatry Association, 1975); "Emotional Problems and Psychopharmacology," Audio-Digest Foundation, *Family Practice*, vol. 25, no. 29 (Aug. 1, 1977); Carl P. Malquist, "Childhood Depressions," Weekly Psychiatry Update Series #36 (Biomedia, 1977); William Zung, "The Pharmacology of Disordered Sleep," *Journal of the American Medical Association* 211 (March 2, 1970).

Chapter 15
How Do You Handle Anxiety?

1. Gary R. Collins, *Overcoming Anxiety* (Santa Ana, CA: Vision House Publishers, 1973).

2. W. E. Vine, *Expository Dictionary of New Testament Words* (Old Tappan, NJ: Fleming H. Revell, 1966); Robert Young, *Young's Analytical Concordance to the Bible* (Grand Rapids: Eerdmans, 1970).

Chapter 16
How Do You Find Lifelong Happiness?

1. Kenneth F. Weaver, "The Incredible Universe," *National Geographic* 145 (1974): 589-625.

2. Shannon and Backus, "The Psychodynamics of Depression," *Journal of the Arkansas Medical Society*, December, 1973.

3. Robert E. Grinder, *Studies in Adolescence: A Book of Readings in Adolescent Development*, third edition (New York: Macmillan, 1975).

4. Shannon and Backus, "Depression," *Journal of the Arkansas Medical Society*, July, 1973.

5. Ibid.

6. Ibid.

7. Frank B. Minirth, *Christian Psychiatry* (Old Tappan, NJ: Fleming H. Revell, 1977), pp. 162-165.

Appendix 1
Classifications of Depression

1. Shannon and Backus, "Depression," *Journal of the Arkansas Medical Society*, July, 1973.

2. Ibid.

3. Ibid.

4. *Diagnostic and Statistical Manual of Mental Disorders*, second edition (Washington, DC: American Psychiatric Association, 1968).

Appendix 2
Case Studies of Depressed Individuals

1. Shannon and Backus, "Treatment of Depression," *Journal of the Arkansas Medical Society*, January, 1974.

Appendix 3
Drugs and the Treatment of Depression

1. John M. Davis, "Overview: Maintenance Therapy in Psychiatry: II. Affective Disorders," *American Journal of Psychiatry*, vol. 133, no. 1 (Jan. 1976): 1; Joe Mendels, "Lithium in the Treatment of Depression," *American Journal of Psychiatry*, vol. 133, no. 4 (April 1976): 373; Prakash G. Ettigi and Gregory M. Brown, "Psychoneuroendocrinology of Affective Disorders: An Overview," *American Journal of Psychiatry*, vol. 134, no. 5 (May 1977): 493; "Emotional Problems and Psychopharmacology," Audio-Digest Foundation, *Family Prac-*

tice, vol. 25, no. 29 (Aug. 1, 1977); "Treatment with Psychotropic Drugs," Audio-Digest Foundation, *Psychiatry*, vol. 4, no. 19 (Oct. 13, 1975); "Management of Treatment-Resistant Depression," Audio-Digest Foundation, *Psychiatry*, vol. 5, no. 18 (Sept. 20, 1976); "Biological Dimensions in Psychiatry," Audio-Digest Foundation, *Psychiatry*, vol. 6, no. 1 (Jan. 10, 1977); "Drug Actions and Interactions," Audio-Digest Foundation, *Psychiatry*, vol. 6, no. 7 (April 11, 1977); "Models of Affective Disorders," *Neuropsychopharmacology*, no. 6 in a series (1977); John M. Davis, *Depression: A Practical Approach* (New York: Medcom, 1974); Steven Secunda, "Clinical Use of the Monamine Oxidase Inhibitors," Weekly Psychiatry Update Series #11 (Biomedia, 1976); Robert O. Friedel and Robert J. Bielski, "Prediction of Response to Antidepressant Medications," Weekly Psychiatry Update Series #12 (Biomedia, 1977); "Depression," *Psychiatric Annals*, vol. 3, no. 2 (Feb. 1973); *The Neuropharmacology of Depression* (Cincinnati: Merrell-National Laboratories, 1977); James W. Maas, "Biogenic Amines and Depression," *Archives of General Psychiatry*, vol. 32 (Nov. 1975); *Mandates Depression* (New York: Medcom, 1975); Ross J. Baldessarini, *The Basis for Amine Hypotheses in Affective Disorders: A Critical Evaluation* (American Medical Association, 1977); Frank Deleon-Jones et al., *Diagnostic Subgroups of Affective Disorders and Their Urinary Excretion of Catecholamine Metabolites* (American Journal of Psychiatry Association, 1975).

2. David M. Shaw, "Tryptophan," Weekly Psychiatry Update Series #41 (Biomedia, 1977).

3. "Drug Actions and Interactions."

4. Ibid.

5. Ibid.

6. Ibid.

7. Ibid.

8. "Treatment with Psychotropic Drugs."

9. "Current Controversies in Gynecology," Audio-Digest Foundation, *Family Practice*, vol. 25, no. 15 (April 18, 1977).

10. "Controversies in. . .," Audio-Digest Foundation, *Psychiatry*, vol. 6, no. 6 (April 25, 1977).

11. "The Problem Drinker," Audio-Digest Foundation, *Psychiatry*, vol. 6, no. 19 (October 10, 1977).

12. Ibid.

13. Ibid.

14. Ibid.

15. Ibid.

16. John S. Tamerin, "Psychological Aspects of Smoking Cessation," Weekly Psychiatry Update Series #40 (Biomedia, 1977).

17. Hardin Jones and Helen Jones, *Sensual Drugs: Deprivation and Rehabilitation of the Mind* (Cambridge: Cambridge University Press, 1977).

18. Philip Solomon and Vernon D. Patch, *Handbook of Psychiatry*, third edition (Lange Medical Publications, 1974).

19. Michel R. Mandel, "The Contemporary Use of ECT," Weekly Psychiatry Update Series #10 (Biomedia, 1976).

20. Solomon and Patch, *Handbook of Psychiatry*.
21. Ibid.
22. Ibid.

INDICES

1

INDEX OF SCRIPTURE

2

GENERAL INDEX